ECHO
LOBA
LOBA
ECHO

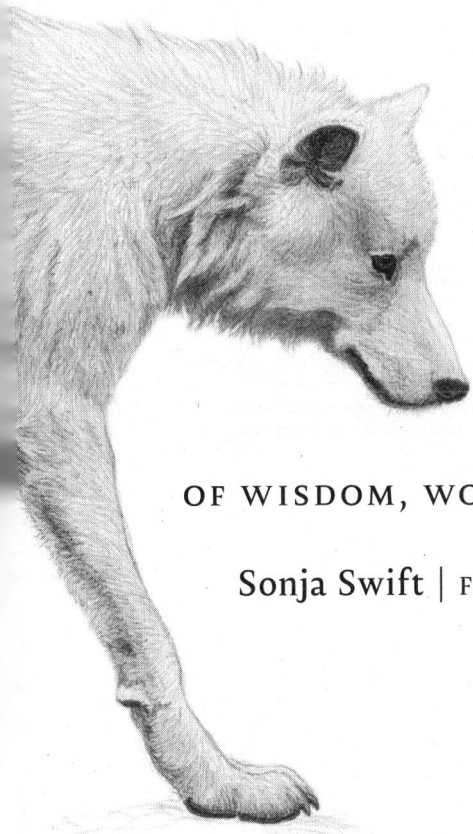

ECHO
LOBA
LOBA
ECHO

OF WISDOM, WOLVES AND WOMEN

Sonja Swift | Foreword by Winona LaDuke

RMB

First Edition

For information on purchasing bulk quantities of this book, or to obtain media excerpts or invite the author to speak at an event, please visit rmbooks.com and select the "Contact" tab.

RMB | Rocky Mountain Books Ltd.
rmbooks.com
@rmbooks
facebook.com/rmbooks

Cataloguing data available from Library and Archives Canada
ISBN 9781771606288 (hardcover)
ISBN 9781771606295 (electronic)

Cover illustration by Naja Abelsen
Design: Lara Minja, Lime Design

Printed and bound in Canada

We would like to take this opportunity to acknowledge the traditional territories upon which we live and work. In Calgary, Alberta, we acknowledge the Niitsítapi (Blackfoot) and the people of the Treaty 7 region in Southern Alberta, which includes the Siksika, the Piikuni, the Kainai, the Tsuut'ina, and the Stoney Nakoda First Nations, including Chiniki, Bearpaw, and Wesley First Nations. The City of Calgary is also home to Métis Nation of Alberta, Region III. In Victoria, British Columbia, we acknowledge the traditional territories of the Lkwungen (Esquimalt and Songhees), Malahat, Pacheedaht, Scia'new, T'Sou-ke, and W̱SÁNEĆ (Pauquachin, Tsartlip, Tsawout, Tseycum) peoples.

We acknowledge the financial support of the Government of Canada through the Canada Book Fund and the Canada Council for the Arts, and of the province of British Columbia through the British Columbia Arts Council and the Book Publishing Tax Credit.

Canada   Canada Council   Conseil des arts   BRITISH   BRITISH COLUMBIA
          for the Arts   du Canada   COLUMBIA   ARTS COUNCIL
                                                           An agency of the Province of British Columbia

Disclaimer
The views expressed in this book are those of the author and do not necessarily reflect those of the publishing company, its staff, or its affiliates.

For Marcus, Zia, and future dreams.

For the wisdom keepers, wayfinders, and misfits.

And for the wolves still alive and singing in the hinterlands

of both territory and soul.

When you are writing you are actually engaging in a spiritual activity. It is a responsibility. That's why they used to kill writers.

—AL YOUNG

Contents

Foreword

LOVE SONG, MA'IINGAN NAAGAMOWIN
Winona LaDuke

It's said that in the beginning of time the Wolf and the Anishinaabe walked side by side. Upon parting, we were instructed, "What befalls the Wolf befalls the Anishinaabe." That is our story.

The Ma'iingan Dodaem is this village of mine, Ne-jingwakokaw-adjiw, or Pine Point, Minnesota. Here the village is full of Ma'iingan and sturgeon *dodaem*, or the Clans. We are from these relatives *omaa akiing*, here on this land. The Anishinaabe remember and are guided by the wolves. "In our area, this sacred relationship is alive and well. The wolf is still instructing us if you listen," Pebaamibines Dennis Jones has said. "The spirit of the wolf travels with the wind, that's where you can find him. And the spirit of the wolf is still consulted in ceremonies. It's where you ask for direction in your life."

This is a love song to the Wolf, the Grandmother Wolf who just wants to sing. This writing is Sonja Swift's love song to a vilified and persecuted being, a testimony for the erasure, for the generations of hating, and for the animal that remains, from Chernobyl to the Deep North. This writing is also about our own story, drifted far from our original instructions and our relationship to each other and the natural world. A call to return to those instructions. And this writing is a history of humans, our folly and what happens when humans are not there. *Echo Loba, Loba Echo* is ultimately a loving story for her young son, so he may see this world clearly and see how beautiful we once were and how to be those beautiful people once again.

Sonja Swift has traveled far with the sacred being, Ma'iingan the wolf. From Inuit territory in Greenland to Dene territory, she has seated herself humbly at the table or the fire, pen in hand, until the story is told. I see her drinking tea and smelling of smoked hides, as we do in the North, laughing, smiling, and listening as a story unfolds. She is a gentle spirit. Patient, like a wolf.

Wolves are the most widely dispersed mammals, besides humans, in the world. She has retraced those paths and stories. And she has followed the story of the relationship between humans and wolves *nopeming*, deep into the woods as well. She has found wolves where they were erased, not unlike the stories of Indigenous Peoples, still present, watching.

She found the wolves, or more likely they have found her, asking that their story be retold, the story of how they have been here, like the peoples. She finds wolves in places where they are not remembered: skulls at the La Brea Tar Pits and reminders of the great wolf kills in California, bountied like Indians, and killed, as our ancestors would warn us, in the same ways.

Seeking a thread that has escaped, Swift finds the lead and follows, pulling down stories from the small references in history to weave a deeper understanding. In skillful prose she takes us from the depths of vengeful history to the great stories of the "barren worlds," where nature writer Hugh Brophy would note the nonpastoral worlds of the north, foreign to European colonizers, where the wolves live. Where there are no white men, there are wolves. Until the white men return again.

Like the woman with the special tool for the invisible ink, she finds the story behind the erasure. She delves into "the mute overlook" of history and reminds us who we are. The brutality of wolves near extinction woven into the same stories of the deaths of millions of women, Indigenous Peoples killed like wolves. The story the same, gut-wrenching, and not so different from the hangings and quarterings of old to those of the killing of wolves.

The cruelty of humans is unbearable.

And yet through this she reminds us of our humanity. She reminds us of the stories of being "raised by the wolves" and beckons us to look at how wolves parent, and finds, indeed, that wolf communities teach us how to raise children – extended families, and to play. These are lessons of Indigenous Peoples, of the Anishinaabeg. The wolf plays 30 percent of the time – that is far better than most humans these days. There's a quality of life in that of the wolf we can remember. We must, however, drop some baggage, let go of the trappings of this material world. And watch; we can learn.

In these times when technological man is failing, she takes us to the places left by man and now taken over by wolves. She takes us to Chernobyl, where the wolves have returned, rewilding the places abandoned by disaster. While scientists watch over the genetic mutations these wolves will carry on, there is indeed amazement at their return and their resilience. Life wishes to continue, and as man retreats, homelands are taken back by the wild. Indeed, life returns, as the wolves have, not only in the exclusion zone of Chernobyl but in the return of the polar bears to the northern Russian military posts. When humans are gone, the animals return. Life comes back. There's a deep lesson in that.

It's said that, on a worldwide scale, Indigenous Peoples comprise 4 percent of the world's people but live with 75 percent of the world's biodiversity. We live where the Wild Things are. The invasions to our territories continue, from the Amazon to the Deep North, and we continue our resistance, as it is not only a resistance for the Native People, but it is a resistance for the animals, the four-legged, the winged, those with fins, and those with roots. As relatives, we understand they have no commanding voice, and we are their voice. We are, after all, relatives.

As for my people, we still stand for the wolves. The Anishinaabe have not forgotten our instructions and our teachings. The wolves live with us – some 19 reservations in the northern part of Michigan, Wisconsin, Minnesota, North Dakota, and Montana are Anishinaabe, and that's not surprisingly much of the remaining home of the timber wolf. Tribal governments across Minnesota's wolf range declared reservations off limits to hunting in 2012 after the federal authorities removed Endangered Species Act protections for wolves and turned over management to the states. The Red Lake Band took it a step further, naming the tribe's 846,000-acre forest a wolf sanctuary. In 2021, politicized by the hunting industry, which insists that wolves take "their deer," Wisconsin reopened the wolf hunts, killing some 500 animals in two short years. In response, six Anishinaabe tribes are suing Wisconsin, noting that the wolf hunt is counter to the Treaty Rights protected in the *Voight* decision and the subsequent *Mille Lacs* decision at the US Supreme Court. We understand that our ancestors, like our Water Protectors today, protect the wolves and the waters they drink.

Here, Giiwedinong, where the Anishinaabe and wolf live, you can hear the relatives howling, sometimes just to do so. To hear their own voices, loud and clear and present, resounding and echoing in the North. In this time of the sixth mass extinction, how do we return wolves, how do we return with our children and grandchildren? With love and prayer.

That is what we have. Love, prayer, and good work for this love, this relative. That is really Sonja's gift in this writing; she has written a love song. Ma'iingan Naagamowin. A Love Song to the Wolf.

Preface

The vision for this book was first glimpsed like a sun dog. On a road trip going the long way from the west coast of California to the Black Hills in South Dakota. North, east, and then south. Traversing the west. Traveling with *Of Wolves and Men* in my lap. Thinking about my life as a woman. Crossing the border at Glacier, Montana, into Waterton Lakes, Alberta, where I encountered the Rocky Mountain Books logo on the back of *The Homeward Wolf.* Visiting Head-Smashed-In Buffalo Jump in the Alberta Plains. Cypress Hills to Thunder Bay to Lake Nipigon, where en route I touched a wolf pelt hanging in the backroom of a trading post. Making a stopover at White Earth, Minnesota, and visiting Winona there, learning the Ojibwe word for wolf.

This particular vision didn't dissipate. It rooted itself in my imagination, and I owed it to myself to follow the tracks in the snow. I also owed it to the wolves. The vision being a story about wolves and women, yet something else also, something about how people are mirrored in the metaphor of Wolf. A metaphor that embodies worldviews colliding, and the collision, the fallout, we live with still. Here in North America and across the world. A metaphor that also embodies wisdom for how to live. Of course, I have written about wolves directly as well, their own cultures, survival stories, acts of rebellion, and vital roles in maintaining healthy territories. Only I saw something worth telling in addition to these accounts, of which much has already been written. And I found out quickly that there were many associations to weave together, including complex meanings embedded in what is often associated with wolves (and women) – the concept of *wild*. In all these ways, the story became prismatic.

I was nine months pregnant with my son when I completed my MFA in creative writing with an early draft of this book, and gave birth to him at home less than two weeks later. The vision for this story began when I imagined becoming a mother, and was seen through to completion across the early years of motherhood. I name this because it is a central undercurrent to the story. The love of a mother for her child, the love of a woman for the world her child is inheriting. Wolves are known mothers, protectors, fiercely devoted. I also nearly gave up on the manuscript. Not because of motherhood, as some might assume, but because I was sidelined by shouldering unforeseen work responsibilities and lost sight of my artist path. The crucial moment was returning to the manuscript, reading it with fresh eyes, and seeing my commitment through.

All along I knew the form would be unusual, but I didn't quite know how until it all finally, intuitively, came together. This is hybrid creative nonfiction, a collage of prose and poetry. This is a personal story and an extensively researched account. (I now have a bookshelf dedicated to books wholly about wolves, and yet those are not my only sources.) This is also a compilation of stories people have generously shared with me. If there is a peculiar theme stitched across these pages, it is perhaps my dedication to expanding and complicating and upending my comprehension of the world. A keenness to perceive differently, to understand more fully, especially from the Original Peoples of the land. In reading this book, I invite you to as well.

Acknowledgements

The making of this book draws on many people's wisdom, including that of the land and animals. This means my gratitude extends far beyond what I can adequately name here.

I thank the publishers where excerpts of this book previously appeared: Deconstructed Artichoke Press, which published *Alphabet Atlas*, my first chapbook of prose poems; True Story, an imprint of Creative Nonfiction, which published *Tarot of Transformation*, a series of vignettes structured on the tarot deck's Major Arcana; *Langscape Magazine*, a Terralingua publication, which published the photo essay "Mirroring the Land: Biocultural Diversity Embodied"; *Madrona Project #3* by Empty Bowl, which published the poem "Paw"; and the art & lit zine *Rag #7* by Cassandra Rockwood-Rice, which published an earlier version of the poem "Language Born of Territory."

To those of you who reviewed one of the many drafts in the making, thank you: Judith Serin, who saw this in its earliest iterations, for your consistent kindness and support. Tonya Foster, for inspiring me to make this piece strange. Caroline Goodwin, for expressly valuing the narrative of the personal journey. Shin Yu Pai, for your encouragement and writer's advice right when I needed it. Chip Livingston, for your unequivocal love of canines and spot-on edits. A-dae Romero-Briones, for sharing your cultural knowledge and poignant observations. Sabrina Barreto, for being so generously affirming. Kirsten Craven, for your thorough copy edits and patience as I carefully let the manuscript go. And Seema Reza for sharing notes on all that it takes to see this through.

Special thanks to everyone, friends and strangers alike, whose stories, scholarship, and perspectives are woven into this book. To the authors, poets, and storytellers quoted or referenced herein, I thank you. In particular, sincere gratitude to Robert Shimek, Winona LaDuke, Jeannette Armstrong, Lorraine Nez, A-dae Romero-Briones, Dave de Wit, Itoah Scott-Enns, Alejandro Argumedo, Tonya Foster, Sonja Holy Eagle, Ellie Epp, Liisi Egede Hegelund, Cassandra Smithies, Katelyn Newman, Lilian Hill, and Katsi Cook. A tribute goes to Al Young, who has since walked on into the great "Blues" yonder.

Heartfelt acknowledgement goes to my family on both sides of the Atlantic Ocean, and my ancestors.

Thank you to Don Gorman and Rocky Mountain Books for seeing the merit of this as another wolf story and something other than that also. Enduring gratitude to the staff at RMB for all your support.

Qujanaq/tak to Naja Abelsen for responding to my inquiry after I finally looked up the artist on the back of my favorite postcard from Nuuk: your illustration of the Arctic wolf, an image that accompanied much of this writing from the corner of my desk.

Mii'gwech to Winona LaDuke for so lovingly complementing your voice and writing with this story, for your courage and lifelong dedication to protecting the water, the wolves, and the wild rice for future generations.

Deep gratitude to Marcus Lund for insisting I return to this project when I'd nearly abandoned it, for sharing your perceptiveness, artistry, humor and sage witness, so many good books, songs, and stories, wayfaring conversations traveling back roads, and for walking beside me all the way through.

Zia Atlas, my beloved son, I wrote this in your honor. May your generation know more stories of courageous returns.

ALLIED WITH WOLF

When I was a child, my American grandmother asked me what animal I wanted her to sponsor on my behalf. A novel kind of Christmas gift. At the Living Desert Zoo and Gardens in Palm Springs, California. I said wolf. She was upset, I was later told, dismayed that I'd pick a predator, *this* predator, not something more sweet and cuddly. But, still, she sent me a card with a photo of the Mexican wolf. I was so proud of that card, and not because she had donated some token money at my request but because I had allied myself with the wolf.

It seems my grandmother, like so many, saw the wolf as a representation of evil. Even though she spent many a summer in McCall, Idaho, in Nez Perce country, a place where wolves are more common than most these days. I saw her as a woman actively covering up her own pain. She always wore salmon-pink lipstick. I self-proclaimed a kind of hatred for the color until recently, when I bought a wide-brimmed ceramic mug on discount, and then it dawned on me that the glaze was a veritable sunset pink. There are mornings when I specifically want to drink my coffee in this cup and this cup only. It is said that the world's first oceans were pink.

The last image I have of Tutu (her self-adopted title for "grandmother" appropriated from the Hawaiʻian language, a culture she was enchanted by in tourist fashion) was in her Indian Wells bedroom. Alone in a giant Spanish-style room, muted light through heavy curtains, her tiny, shrunken body hardly bulged beneath the blankets. Her only company was Keiki, a petite black cat, who made an equally small dent at the far corner beside her. She reminded me of a frail bird, all bone.

Tutu didn't care much to see me at the time, as she was more focused on my father, though she entertained me briefly with a tired smile and held my hand in that fierce grip of hers. Her palm still soft as velvet. I appreciated the realness, the way exhaustion had done away with pretense. Her way of saying she was dying was to remark, "Well, I guess my dancing days are over."

The parting message I took in this moment was simple: dance, girl. Dance as long as you are able. I liked that message. I have held onto this memory as an authentic gift from my grandmother, next to that photo of the Mexican wolf.

WOLF

Noun

1. Wolf (*lupus*) is another word for whore (*lupa*); for woman. Another word for howl, for sing, for hysteric ("of the womb"). Watch out they'll drug you, trap you, strychnine you.

2. Wolf is another word for outcast, scapegoat, black sheep. The one dead lamb and the wolf hunt, greasy bones thrown to the dogs.

3. Wolf is another word for backcountry. Tundra. Blamed for human violence and blood lust, you must go far, far away from roads for safety. And even there the helicopters will find you.

Verb

1. Wolfing is another word for war. In English dialect.

Ahtna Athabascan: *tikaani*
Albanian: *ujk, vjuk*
Algonquin: *mahigan*
Anishinaabe: *ma'iingan*
Apache: *ba'cho, ba'uchaahi, ma'cho*
Arabic: *dhib*
Armenian: *gayl*
Asturiano: *llobu, lloba*
Bulgarian: *walk*
Chemehuevi: *tivaci*
Cherokee: *wahy'a*
Cheyenne: *ho'nene, maiyun*
Chinese: *yitiao lang*
Chinook: *lelou, leloo*
Choctaw: *neshoba*
Croatian: *vuk*
Czech: *vlk*
Dakota: *šunktokeca*
Danish: *ulv*
Dutch: *wolf*
Estonian: *hunt*
Farsi: *gorg*
Finnish: *susi*
French: *loup*
Georgian: *mgeli*
German: *wulf*
Gitano: *orú*

Greek: *lieko, lyk*
Greenland – Inuit: *amarok, amaroq*
Hebrew: *ze'ev*
Hindi: *hundar bheriya*
Hopi: *kweo*
Hungarian: *farkas*
Inuktitut: *singarti*
Iñupiat: *amaguk*
Italian: *lupo*
Irish: *mac tír*
Japanese: *ōkami*
Kanarese: *thola, vraka*
Kiliwa: *mlti' tay, mlti' pelas msaap*
Kiowa: *uy kuy*
Korean: *iri, neuk dae*
Lakota: *šung'manitu tanka*
Latin: *lupus*
Latvian: *vilks*
Lenape: *mohegan, te-me*
Lithuanian: *vilkas*
Malayalam: *chennaya*
M'ikmac: *paqtism*
Mohawk: *mahiingan*
Mongolian: *tchono*
Nahuatl: *cuetlachtli, nexcoyotl*
Navajo: *ma'iitsoh*
Nepali: *bvaso*

Nootka: *lokwa'*

Norwegian: *ulv, ulven*

Ojibwe: *ma'iingan*

Otomí: *gamiñ'o*

Pashto: *levee*

Pawnee: *skiri' ki*

Polish: *wał/wilk*

Pomo (eastern dialect): *çi M éw*

Portuguese: *lobo*

Purhépecha (Tarasco): *jiuatsï*

Romanian: *lup*

Russian: *wolk*

Seminole: *o-ba-ho-she*

Seneka: *kyiyu*

Serbian: *vuk*

Shawnee: *m-weowa*

Shoshone: *beya ish*

Slovakian: *vlk (obyca iny)*

Slovenian: *volk*

Spanish: *lobo, loba*

Swedish: *ulv, varg*

Syilx: *nc'i?cən*

Tamil: *onai*

Tarahumara: *naríbochi, naríwari*

Telugu: *toralu*

Tłįchǫ: *nǫdi*

Tibetan: *bhangi*

Turkish: *kurt*
Ukrainian: *bobk*
Urdu: *bheria*
Ute: *sinapu*
Wet'suwet'en: *yis*
Yaqui: *kwewu*[1]

1   The majority of this list comes from "'Wolf' in Different Languages," Wolf
     Song of Alaska, www.wolfsongalaska.org, with alphabets and languages I
     added. Jeannette Armstrong shared the Syilx word, which is naming the wolf's
     own language with which it speaks. David de Wit shared the Wet'suwet'en
     word, which is for timber wolf. A-dae Romero Briones corrected the spelling
     of the Pomo word and specified the dialect.

Echo: sound of snowfall

temple mantra
singing bowl

Loba:
sound
of

singing

echo

echo

echo

echo

ONE WHO GUIDES THE WAY

I met Robert Shimek at the White Earth Land Recovery Project and Honor the Earth headquarters in northern Minnesota. *Gaa-waabaabiganikaag Anishinaabeg* (People from where there is an abundance of white clay), the White Earth Ojibwe Nation. My husband Marcus and I were stopping by on a road trip to visit our friend Winona LaDuke. The last time we'd been here, pink corn hung in the rafters. This time it was late summer, pushing autumn. Upon pulling into the parking lot of the old converted school grounds that are now hub for two nonprofits; a daycare; Native Harvest wild rice, maple syrup, and heritage corn processing; and Niijii radio, I noticed the newly painted mural on the concrete wall next to their windmill, of wolves. When I told Winona I'd been reading Barry Lopez's book *Of Wolves and Men* en route, she walked us inside a community room and sat us down with Bob. "If you want to talk about wolves, he's your man."

Bob launched right into story. Started off by telling us about the first wolf he ever saw as a boy. A red wolf. Tall as him at the time. And the five wolf pups he found in the woods once, emaciated and tangled up in a bundle for warmth. How he just couldn't stand leaving them to die. So he started to bring them dog food soaked in water, made soft, and then later, road kill. All through the summer he fed this litter of wolf pups until they grew strong and set off roaming.

He knew a wolf pack could be gone as long as six weeks traversing their territory before showing back up again. So he waited, patiently, until the end of September when, on a late afternoon with the daylight fading, he heard an alpha howl and the pups responding. He timed their return within days. They'd found an alpha, a loner, to lead them; teach them how to live. All five pups survived that first winter. He says this, beaming. Speaking slowly and methodically, with a strong sense of tradition and careful word choice, he pauses to recall or let things sink in, serious, and then in a flash smiles wide for the joy of what he just shared.

He told us about the advocacy work, the endangered species protection wolves have had and then lost, and how the Ojibwe tribes stand united in making wolves welcome, given safe haven, on their territories. Currently, there are a couple million acres of Ojibwe land proclaimed wolf sanctuary, but the state of Minnesota doesn't want to acknowledge it.

Bob quoted a friend who once said, "If the lynx go away I cease to exist," admiring the simplicity and directness of the statement, the deep truth of it. "It is that way for us Ojibwe and wolves."

To which he shared his experience in a vision fast years ago. For four days and four nights he fasted alone in a hand-built lodge. Beginning on the first night, things started happening in terms of the supernatural, for which English is short on suitable words, with the wolf pack visiting on and off throughout. By the last day he'd lost track of time, knowing simply it was the day he'd leave, take down the lodge and be picked up. There was daylight, but he couldn't tell the hour, and though he considered taking down the lodge various times, some sense to wait told him not to. Then it rained, and he was glad for the shelter. After the rain stopped, Bob describes lying in the lodge watching drops of water fall to the ground, and that was when the wolf appeared. Wolf walked within arm's length of him and pissed right by the side of his head. Three squirts. He kicked his head back laughing when he told me this, saying distinctly, "I was accepted!" By the time the trees had dried from the warmth of sun that followed the rainstorm, he took down the lodge and, with impeccable timing, his friends arrived to pick him up.

The Ojibwe word for wolf is *ma'iingan*. The one sent here by that all-loving spirit to show us the way.[2] In other words, guide.

Bob said for years he asked people about the true meaning of ma'iingan. Wolf, they'd say. To which he'd shake his head, yeah, I know, but what does it really mean? "So many of our words are just loaded with deep meaning," he told me on a phone call, reflecting how it wasn't until he met an Elder from Red Lake who answered his question with "when we say that word Ma'iingan, we are invoking the one put here by that all-loving spirit to show us the way." Everything has a small creation story, Bob explained, which is why the red ash, spruce, walleye, and all else exist. "But of the wolf, there is no creation story, wolf has been here since the beginning."[3] Wolf taught the people how to live. And for many years wolves and people roamed the earth together as companions.

Larry Still Day "Big Wolf," from the neighboring Miskwaagamiiwizaaga'igan Red Lake Nation, has said simply, "There is no spiritual

2   "Ma'iingan (The Wolf) Our Brother," White Earth Land Recovery Project, http://welrp.org/maiingan-the-wolf-our-brother.
3   Robert Shimek, personal communication with author, Honor the Earth headquarters, White Earth, Minnesota, September 2015.

separation between us and wolf."[4] Although there is a prophecy that says, one day, wolves and people would go separate ways, and chaos would reign. That time is now.

The Ainu, Indigenous People of the island of Hokkaido in northern Japan, once believed their people came from the union of a wolf-like canine and a goddess. Their stories also tell of male wolves taking human brides, and female wolves becoming the wives or concubines of Ainu Chiefs.[5] Ainu poetry celebrated the wolf, and some Ainu communities would also sacrifice wolves, as well as bears and owls, in *iomante*, or "sending away" ceremonies. They considered wolves to be their gods, their ancestors.[6] Wolf was known as the high-ranking god, Horkew Kamuy, "howling god."[7]

The haggard, one-eyed, long-bearded, wanderer Odin, a Norse god, had two wolves at his side: Geri and Freki. They accompanied him in battle alongside his two ravens. Loki, the Viking trickster god of dawn, fathered Fenris, the wolf.[8] Hyrrokin, in Nordic mythology, is a giantess. She rides astride a giant gray wolf, with eyes like two moons, and a snake around his head for a bridle. Gray wolf-horse of the giantesses. Night rider.[9]

Joe Martin, Tla-o-quia-aht master canoe carver from the west coast of Vancouver Island, in so-called British Columbia, describes the wolf crest as among "the most important of the animals," often at

4   Julia Huffman, *Medicine of the Wolf* (Cleveland, OH: Gravitas Ventures, 2015), eVideo.
5   Brett Walker, *The Lost Wolves of Japan* (Seattle: University of Washington Press, 2009).
6   Walker, *The Lost Wolves of Japan*.
7   Walker, 83.
8   Barry Lopez, *Of Wolves and Men* (New York: Scribner, 1978).
9   Lopez.

the bottom of the totem pole, as the base, because they "uphold the natural law."[10]

The Pawnee, a Plains tribe nowadays located in Oklahoma, have a language of hand signs. The signal for wolf is a *U* formed by the second and third fingers of the right hand, held up next to the right ear, then brought forward. The same hand signal also means Pawnee.[11] To this day, the wolf figures prominently on the Great Seal of the Pawnee Nation.

Animals have souls and are capable of rational thought, said La Fontaine to Descartes. His was a voice isolated in an era of great and unforgivable forgetting, a voice in profound disagreement with Cartesian dualism, "beast machines," animal as lesser than, body and mind as separate, and woman as inferior in the superiority of thought. All false, yet all of which perpetuated brutal metaphorical segregation and caused a dissecting of the fabric and intelligence of life.

metaphor (n.)
from Greek *metaphora*, literally "a carrying over," from meta "over, across" + *pherein* "to carry, bear" (from PIE root **bher* – to carry," also "to bear children."[12]

I stand with La Fontaine. I see Earth on the back of Turtle. Time in the eyes of Whale. And kinship with Wolf.

---

10   David Moskowitz, *Wolves in the Land of Salmon* (Portland, OR: Timber Press, 2013), 237.
11   Candace Savage, *Wolves* (Vancouver, BC: Douglas & McIntyre, 1995).
12   Taken in part from the *Online Etymology Dictionary*, https://www.etymonline.com/word/metaphor.

Loba: scent of spruce sap

warm heart
sinew

IF YOU LOOK LIKE A WOLF

Once the most widely distributed land mammal in the world (next to people), today wolves are mostly extinct across their home terrain, their natural range. Northern latitudes. Half of the world. Extinct, from Latin, "to quench," as in flames, a fire extinguished.

The cause of their disappearance: systemic use of poison, trapping, net, hook, snare, bullet, bait. Strychnine used indiscriminately, with the covert permission of governments, by men making money as trappers or otherwise for sport. Killing for the sake of it. Spread across areas so large that entire populations of foxes, wolverines, and wolves, alongside any other meat eaters, were wiped out. Poisoned wolves, foxes, or coyotes slobber upon the grass, sick and gagging, and coat grass blades with the same venom killing them from inside. Once sun-dried, the poisonous properties hold a long time, causing death months or even years later to horse, antelope, buffalo, deer, or migratory bird.[13]

Strychnine: death by convulsion.

Predator management to this day includes flying helicopters, aerial shooting, setting cyanide ejectors, hiding traps, and using ambush and sniper tactics.[14] Sounds a lot like war. A former US Wildlife Services trapper exposed the Wyoming Department of Agriculture

---

13   Lopez, *Of Wolves and Men*.
14   Brenda Peterson, *Wolf Nation: The Life, Death and Return of Wild American Wolves* (Philadelphia, PA: Da Capo Press, 2017).

for using poisons banned since the 1970s to sell to predator control boards and ranchers.[15]

Wildlife Services is an obscure agency. Its mandate reads deceitfully: "to resolve wildlife conflicts to allow people and wildlife to coexist." What this actually means is it kills animals, most often to protect interests of select ranchers and game hunters.[16] Its trappers are specifically responsible for killing "problem" predators. "Simply put, it is the hired gun of the livestock industry."[17] In 2021 alone, more than 1.75 million animals across the United States were killed, at a rate of about 200 animals every hour.[18] Both intentionally and unintentionally, considering the methods they continue to use: traps, snares, and poisons, as well as gassing or shooting from helicopters.

There is another Wildlife Services strategy officially called "collaring for later control," whereby what is known as "Judas" wolves are used, wolves who are collared so they can lead helicopters to their pack. The sharpshooters kill as many wolves as they can and leave the collared wolf to lead them to the next pack, hoping the wolf will join up with other wolves or form a new pack, after the loss of their family. These Judas wolves can go years watching their pack die and forming another, oblivious that they are leading the helicopters back again.[19]

15   Peterson.
16   Peterson.
17   Carter Niemeyer, *Wolf Land* (Boise, ID: BottleFly Press, 2016), 17.
18   Oliver Milman, "'A Barbaric Federal Program': US Killed 1.75m Animals Last Year – or 200 per Hour," *The Guardian*, March 25, 2022, https://www.theguardian.com/world/2022/mar/25/us-government-wildlife-services-animals-deaths.
19   Peterson, *Wolf Nation*.

Canadian author Farley Mowat's book *Never Cry Wolf* was published in 1963. Two years earlier, the tourist bureau of the Government of Canada had decided that barren-ground caribou would be the perfect bait to lure trophy hunters in from the United States on subarctic safaris. It was simple. During their winter sojourn, caribou feed in the woods at dawn and dusk and otherwise spend the day atop the ice of open lakes. Choose a lake with a large band of caribou. Fly a safari aircraft to this lake. Circle the band at low altitude, and bunch up the deer into a tight, nervous mob. Land and taxi more circles around the now panic-stricken herd, and unleash a steady fire. Kill enough deer to make sure there are a few good trophies to select from the pile of carcasses afterwards. Cut some quarters to toss in the plane and eat at home days later while antlers are mounted onto a living room wall.

In many cultures, hunting is highly respected, with respect for the animals killed and the act of taking life itself as well. Hunting takes skill, with a covenant of offering gratitude and respect for nourishment. Trophy hunting, by comparison, is a coward's game. Low-flying aircraft or a highly maneuverable helicopter pursuing wolves over frozen tundra while the wolf pack runs desperately. Nowhere to hide, they eventually collapse and die of sheer exhaustion before a blast of buckshot penetrates their tired body.

The "hunter" exits from the helicopter to pick up his prize. Hunters kill for food, not show or laziness, never to waste. And though the meaning differs, the word remains the same.

Wolves don't hunt for fun like men do. A healthy caribou can outrun a wolf easily. Same goes for deer, moose, elk. Bison or muskox will circle their calves and face wolves head-on. Rather, wolves chase for fun and to test the strength of a herd. They will not seriously try to hunt even a three-week-old fawn. To test a herd by rushing a band and putting it into flight mode shows the wolves the weak, sick, or old. When elk or caribou herds grow stronger, as a result of wolves' presence in the terrain, then they are harder to hunt and wolf populations decrease. Balance.

This all makes sense when there are herds. In the North, caribou numbers continue to dwindle. When caribou herds are scarce then wolves change strategies. For instance, driving a small herd into an ambush where other wolves are waiting, which in any case would still reveal the weaker animals. Once a kill is made, wolves rarely hunt again until the supply of food is entirely gone and the force of hunger compels them to. Wolves have killed more than they can eat only when something was confusing, out of sync. Otherwise, killing is a conversation with the sick elk, the old caribou, the lame buffalo.

Consider this scene: Two bison bulls and two cows lying in the grass. Three in good health, one lame. Wolves approach. The healthy bison ignore them, sauntering away, while the lame one sitting on the ground becomes agitated. By the time a wolf is standing within some 20 feet, this wounded bison rises, legs shaking, to face the wolves alone.[20] There is a relationship here, between predator and prey, between hunter and grass eater, between life and death. I would say more explicitly that there is a protocol, an understanding.

Nevertheless, from Scandinavia to Portugal, Iran to Nepal, and across North America, wolves have been killed with uncanny fury. In North America, northern Canada and Alaska in particular, wolves still have some strongholds. In Eurasia their numbers have

20   Lopez, *Of Wolves and Men*.

more seriously declined. For the most part, wolves exist in small, scattered populations, and while in some regions they are making a comeback, there are many countries where little is known about how they fare, and there is no official regard for their long-term survival.

According to the International Wolf Center, there are estimates of roughly 100,000 wolves across all of Asia, approximately 50,000 in Canada, some 10,000 in Alaska and 5,000 in the continental US, 13,000 in Europe, perhaps 50 in Greenland (depending on whether they happen to be on Ellesmere Island in Canada, or the North, or otherwise east of Greenland, as they wander back and forth),[21] 1 confirmed Mexican gray wolf in Mexico, and "status unknown" in Africa.[22] Although that may well change as the Ethiopian wolf, once thought to be a jackal, has recently been deemed a "new species" of wolf.[23]

It has been asked of the Tasmanian wolf, *Thylacinus cynocephalus*, were they wolves or tigers? While resembling a wolf, with tiger stripes on its back and tail, the so-called tiger-wolf was a marsupial and more closely related to kangaroos, with even a pouch to carry offspring. The Tasmanian tiger-wolf went extinct on the mainland of Australia with the introduction of the dingo, but survived on the island of Tasmania off the south coast of Australia until Europeans arrived. Colonists cleared the land for sheep farming, and come the mid-1800s, landowners and then the government paid bounty for killing tiger-wolves. Poisoned, shot, snared, hunted with dogs,

21   A correction made by Naja Abelsen.
22   "Wolves of the World," International Wolf Center, http://www.wolf.org/wow/world/.
23   "Ethiopia at a Glance," International Wolf Center, https://wolf.org/wow/africa/ethiopia/.

trapped, and otherwise exterminated through the early 1900s. The last known tiger-wolf died in captivity in 1936.[24]

The red wolf, named for its cinnamon-rose fur, is another of the most endangered in the Canidae family. Once common throughout the eastern and south central United States, red wolf populations were decimated in the early part of the 20th century by the same forces. As of writing, fewer than 15 red wolves roam their native habitats in eastern North Carolina,[25] while some 200 red wolves live in captive breeding facilities across the country. I had to correct the figure from 50 to 15 while writing this book.

South America's largest canid is the maned wolf. Today, limited mostly to Brazil's Cerrado, a vast and also threatened savanna because of relentless conversion to commodity crops, and also often forgotten by environmentalists the way the tapestry of grasslands gets overlooked next to the appeal of tall forests. Nicknamed "fox on stilts," and known for a "roar-bark," the maned wolf has the body of a wolf, the face of a fox, and the legs of a fawn, and, apparently, urine that smells like marijuana. Maned wolves travel alone. They are also not wolves but more akin to a wild dog, and with their own genus, *Chrysocyon*. But the common name and the wolf-like face have associated this fruit-eating rodent hunter with the reputation of *el lobo*.[26]

Once worshiped as sacred animals throughout the archipelago of Japan, with upland villagers leaving ceremonial dishes of red beans

24   "Tasmanian Tiger-Wolf," Bagheera, https://www.bagheera.com/tasmanian-wolf/.
25   "Wild Red Wolves Extinction," Environmental Action, https://environmental-action.org/action/wild-red-wolves-extinction/.
26   Sean Mowbray, "The Maned Wolf: Saving South America's Largest Canid," Mongabay, December 7, 2015, https://news.mongabay.com/2015/12/the-maned-wolf-saving-south-americas-unfortunately-named-canid/.

and rice next to wolf dens as offerings to these "large-mouthed" gods, today wolves are extinct from Japan.[27] Where they used to be relied upon to deter wild boar and deer from farmers' prized shiitake mushroom crops, today people use macaque deterrents called *bakuonki* that ignite a natural gas explosion set on a timer, setting off up to five or six explosions in an hour.[28]

As recent as 2021, Idaho expanded wolf killing to 90 percent of the state's wolves.[29] Accomplishing this objective would involve giving wolf hunters rights to do things currently illegal: hunting with night vision goggles, and using snowmobiles or ATVs to chase them down.[30] Montana attempted to pass similar laws, to please certain ranchers and piss off anyone who doesn't share the naive wolf-as-vermin narrative. But after 23 wolves were killed roaming into Montana outside the boundaries of Yellowstone National Park (the most wolves killed in a single season since they were restored to the US northern Rocky Mountains more than 25 years ago), public outcry pressured the state to take a step back and halt the fervor, but only for so long.[31] In late 2022, a Montana judge upheld Republican Governor Greg Gianforte's legislation that calls for the killing of at least 450 wolves, almost 40 percent

27   Walker, *The Lost Wolves of Japan*.

28   Walker.

29   Keith Ridler, "Idaho Wolf Control Board Will Have $1 Million to Kill Wolves," *AP News*, January 19, 2022, https://apnews.com/article/lifestyle-business-idaho-environment-and-nature-wolves-8f73e6664bfdcdc8421e20ba7c28aa98.

30   Troy Oppie, "New Idaho Law Calls for Killing 90% of the State's Wolves," *NPR*, May 21, 2021, https://www.npr.org/2021/05/21/999084965/new-idaho-law-calls-for-killing-90-of-states-wolves.

31   Matthew Brown, "Montana Curbs Wolf Hunt after 23 from Yellowstone Killed," *Associated Press*, January 28, 2022, https://abcnews.go.com/Technology/wireStory/montana-weighs-wolf-hunt-limits-23-yellowstone-killed-82537107.

of Montana's estimated population.[32] (Gianforte is an east coast tech businessman who has bragged about entertaining investment bankers at his Montana home and serving up mountain lion for dinner).[33]

Around the same time, to the east, across the North Atlantic Ocean, Norway lifted a cull injunction to allow killing wolves within its own supposed wolf zone. With fewer than 80 wolves in this oil-rich country, where farmers are subsidized simply to keep people on the land, wolves are targeted yet again. All the while, neighboring Sweden doubled its annual wolf cull in its largest wolf hunt in recent history.[34] And in Germany, after a wolf ate European Commission President Ursula von der Leyen's 30-year-old prized pony, von der Leyen promptly ordered a re-evaluation of the rules protecting wolves across the whole of Europe.[35]

Wolves, it is said, are the most persecuted animals in the world, with the most distorted reputation.

Wolves, it is said, taught people how to live.

Until people forgot.

32 Ryan Devereaux, "Montana Judge Won't Halt Gov. Greg Gianforte's Aggressive Wolf Hunt," The Intercept, November 30, 2022, https://theintercept.com/2022/11/30/wolf-hunt-montana-judge/.

33 "Greg Gianforte," Wikipedia, https://en.wikipedia.org/wiki/Greg_Gianforte.

34 Jon Henley, "Hunters Shoot Dead 54 Wolves in Sweden's Largest Ever Cull," The Guardian, February 7, 2023, https://www.theguardian.com/world/2023/feb/07/swedish-hunters-shoot-dead-54-wolves-in-largest-cull-ever-in-country.

35 Matthew Karnitschnig and Gabriel Rinaldi, "Ursula Takes on the Big Bad Wolf," Politico, January 2, 2023, https://www.politico.eu/article/ursula-takes-on-the-big-bad-wolf/.

It wasn't the end of the world...but you could see it from there.

—JAMES WELCH, THE DEATH OF JIM LONEY

WORLDVIEWS COLLIDING

The last known wolf reportedly killed in England was in the early 16th century, and across most of Europe wolves had been exterminated or reduced to scattered "remnant" populations by 1700.[36] "King Edgar the 'Peaceful of England' let men pay their taxes in the tenth century in wolf heads and their legal fines in wolf tongues."[37] In the United Kingdom today, fierce arguments carry on over whether wolves should ever be reintroduced.[38] Having obliterated their wild animals centuries ago, it seems the tameness of managed gardens and farmed fields has done something to imagination also.

In 17th-century Scotland, people burned the forests to rid the country of wolves. Today, Scotland has 1 percent of its original forest intact.[39] Similarly, in the UK and Ireland, and to varying degrees elsewhere across Europe. European colonists to North America, having grown accustomed to lands devoid of wolves across the recent generations, didn't bother to fence in their sheep or cows. Opting

36   Moskowitz, *Wolves in the Land of Salmon*.
37   Lopez, *Of Wolves and Men*, 147.
38   Helena Horton, "Wolves Shot in Norway after Court Overturns Stay of Execution," *The Guardian*, February 15, 2022, https://www.theguardian.com/world/2022/feb/15/wolves-shot-norway-cull-conservation-zone.
39   Moskowitz, *Wolves in the Land of Salmon*.

to kill rather than oversee their own herds was a peculiar kind of laziness, also a foreigner's imposition of dominance, control.

Rick McIntyre, veteran biological technician for the Yellowstone Wolf Project, is of Scottish heritage. His Glen Noe highland ancestors were, like many Scots, forced by the British to work as wolf killers for the conquering British upper class. In the preface to his book *War against the Wolf*, aptly titled "Witness to Ecological Murder," he writes, "The last Highland wolf reportedly was destroyed in 1743...The thanks my ancestors received for their diligent wolf control was the loss of their land to sheep."[40]

McIntyre made a visit to Shaktoolik in 1993, an Alaskan Iñupiat village along the Bering Strait, to talk about predators with high school students. He showed historic slides of the thousands of wolves killed by strychnine. The students were shocked. Born to a hunting culture, many of them hunters themselves, this was something else altogether. One of the boys asked McIntyre plainly: "Why did they want to kill off *all* the wolves?" The simple question caused McIntyre to realize just how foreign the concept of all-out destruction was to these young Inupiat, while he himself had come to take it for granted that people act this way. Of the student's question, he reflected, "None of it related to the reality of his world, a Native American world of traditions, ethics, and morals that set limits on what humanity can do to fellow forms of life."[41]

European colonists to North America, heavily steeped in this history and wolf lore, brought it with them. Many of the colonists, arriving mostly in the 1800s, wouldn't have had actual experiences

40   Peterson, *Wolf Nation*, 56.
41   Peterson, 6.

with wolves, considering they had been largely eliminated from their homelands years before they set sail. This is a most dangerous mindset, when something is not rooted in personal experience but fabrication, hyped up and sensationalized.

The wolves these colonists encountered when they arrived here were behaviorally conditioned by 10,000 years of peaceful relations with the original people of this continent. Those who took pause to witness, not shoot, wrote of how trusting wolves were, trotting alongside their horses, sitting curiously on a sandbar as people passed by in boats a few feet away.[42]

This is at the center of something grave. What newcomers met here they – the dominant majority, that is – for some reason simply couldn't accept. Whether how bountiful and abundant life was – the phenomenal bison herds, rivers dense with salmon, ancient old-growth forests – or how well the locals could relate to the other original inhabitants.

Town of Craig, Colorado. I enter an army supply store following a dogged woman who has marched in determinedly to offer to put the shopkeeper in touch with someone about a "save our elk from wolves" campaign. The shopkeeper politely declines, "I'd rather not get involved in an issue with so much controversy surrounding it." And the woman is on her way.

When the entry bells on the door stop tinkling, I ask about camp stoves and then get to talking about wolves. The shopkeeper shares her ethic plainly: "all animals belong and are put here for a reason,"

42   Dan Flores, *Horizontal Yellow: Nature and History in the Near Southwest* (Albuquerque: University of New Mexico Press, 1999).

and as a hunter herself, she says she also understands pack and herd behavior. Of elk, she tells me that one should never kill a cow elk, because it messes up the leadership. "Elk are essentially a matriarchal society," she says. "Take out the knowledgeable elder and the herd is lost."

The same goes for wolves. Loss of the alpha in a pack has a destabilizing effect on a wolf pack, either causing the pack to split into two or disintegrate into even smaller packs, or otherwise causing the pack to change hunting habits or home range.[43] This can cause even more ruckus for ranchers because wolves without pack leadership are more prone to picking off calves – they lack the know-how of hunting and protocols of living as a pack. There can be a tendency to think of wolves in terms of numbers, "but you can't replace a relationship," she explains with a calm tone of common sense. Wiping out single members from packs wipes out cohesive systems of complex interrelationship.

Standing there, surrounded by camouflage fabric, bush knives, and camping equipment, I thought to myself, why am I so interested in an issue drenched in such controversy? But "issue" isn't even the word, because what wolf really represents is a worldview collision.

The answer may be this simple: I prefer being subject to Earth, rather than subject to [hu]men's ambition for control.

Like wolf.

---

43   Kevin Van Tighem, *The Homeward Wolf* (Victoria, BC: Rocky Mountain Books, 2013).

So the years went by – wolves, words and moons.

–YANNIS RITSOS, *MONOCHORDS*

WOLF GIRL

I was a feral child. I trusted dogs and horses more than most people. The land: reliance. The ocean: solace. Ice-cold North Pacific Ocean. As a 12-year-old sprite, I had to learn how to duck dive my surfboard under, just so, such that the force of swell wouldn't drag me backwards, suck me into churning whitewash. Back then, I was the only girl in the lineup. It dawned on me years later to ask what of this salt song drive to career my smallness into heavy waves? Because, oddly enough, it wasn't just about sport. The ocean became my safe space: roiling, deep blue, salt water. Waves strong as elephants, strong as pillars falling over. Yet water is softer, more malleable, than stone.

That oceanic color blue. *Blue*: another word for soul, for one's own unique raw eccentricity, born as we all are from salt water. *Blue* is a good word for the cellular imprint of gale storms, the experiences of being shaped by them. It is a word for held-in breath, eyes alert, tracking emotion, taut as an arrow at the bow. Blue, another word for void, things unsaid yet sensed as one does a ghost. *Blue* goes to the sunless depths of the midnight zone. It is a word that is a feeling that is a memory that is a pattern, a tether across lifetimes. It's also a kind word for where children find places to hide. In the manes of horses. In the ocean tides.

Of being a misfit, there is this story: I am perhaps 9 years old, a newbie to ballet classes, with intrepid trepidation. Auditions for the Nutcracker, the big wintertime show, are to be held. I deliberate but opt to try for it, like I'd later try out for middle school basketball, never having played a game, because even as a girl I trusted my physical capacity, my embodiment. So I put on my tie-dyed purple tutu, and my dad drives me the half-hour to town to climb the polished wooden stairwell and walk toward the dance hall. Upon approach, I begin to notice all the other girls in pink, all pink, and I freeze like a deer. I don't bolt like one but move rather like a fox, quietly, back outside to the truck, telling my dad we can go home now, tucking my face behind my warm tail.

I play soccer, give up on ballet. Give up on an element of myself, my nature, which is and always has been called to dance. In soccer, I fight. I run with focus, take some of my angst out in this way, though I still learn about my agility and determined strength. Surfing, on the other hand, becomes a sanctuary, oceanic solitude. Ocean and me. This does not mean lonely though, because the land, like the ocean, is good company.

When I think of wolf children, I think of barefoot meanderings, a peculiar kind of solitude, being a misfit, and misunderstanding in relation to other people. I also think of this story about wolf girl.

It is 1835. The month of May. A child is born at the confluence of Dry Creek and Devil's River in what would become the State of Texas ten years later. Her mother dies in childbirth and her father, as the peculiarities of fate would have it, is killed in a thunderstorm at a nearby ranch where he rode off to in search of help. Mollie Pertul Dent and John Dent, newcomers to this land, dead. The baby girl left alone.

Come 1845, and a boy living at San Felipe Springs, present-day Del Rio, reports seeing "a creature" with long windswept hair attacking a herd of goats alongside several wolves "that looked like a naked girl." There are further reports of similar descriptions, and Apache People speak of seeing small footprints next to wolf tracks in the red desert sands. So a hunt is organized. A hunt for the wolf child.

Day three of the hunt: wolf girl is cornered in a canyon, and the wolf with her is driven off, then shot after looping back to attack the pursuing men. She is bound, flame-eyed and growling, and carried to the nearest ranch outpost. They tie her up as they would a bucking horse. Leave her in an empty room alone.

That evening the girl won't stop howling. The men curse her, try to sleep. In the silken shadows, beneath pewter stars, a pack of wolves surround her prison cell. In their slow, deliberate approach they frighten the livestock, and somehow in the midst of hoofed and bleating uproar, she escapes.

The year 1852, and a surveying crew is exploring a new route to El Paso. They report seeing a woman standing on a sandbar overlooking the Rio Grande, high above the confluence with Devil's River. There are two wolf pups at her side. She is never seen again.[44]

This story, akin to the widely known one about Kamala and Amala, is fact. Witnessed, accounted for. Yet there is also a symbolic element at play here, that of the outcast. Wolf child, wolf girl. A quality of being that is at once natural yet does not fit in. Like wolf, the wolf-girl figure is not to be romanticized. It isn't an easy or entirely comfortable hide to wear.

---

44   Retold from a story referenced in Lopez, *Of Wolves and Men*, 243.

To relate to this character is to know an experience of unsettled awkwardness, to question belonging, to veer for the hills. The wolf child/misfit/outcast, in this case, is also only this in relation to the so-called civilized. Silverware from mine shafts. Regiment in the form of breaking, the way horses are "broken." The camp in the forest where the exiled go could also be called a village.

Once, on a late-night drive uphill to the ridgetop home of my childhood, traversing a familiar winding dirt road, stars visible, smell of sagebrush and oak tannin, I reflected out loud to Marcus how this place was my upbringing. How, as a child, I learned to rely on the land and animal companions. "It's why I act like a forest child," I said, only half-kidding. Then, when I jokingly told him he's helped me adapt to more common human behavior, he said something that made me laugh out loud: "So you're Mowgli, raised by wolves, and I'm Baloo."

The recent reproduction of *The Jungle Book* is a colorful film that won an Academy Award for best visual effects and brought to life the animation classic. Upon leaving the theater, there was a stack of posters depicting the verdant jungle and animal protagonists. I took a copy home. Later, at my kitchen table, staring at the scene of Shere Khan (the tiger), Bagheera (the black panther), Kaa (the python), the clan of monkeys with their giant ape leader King Louie, and the rest of the cast, I noticed the illustrator had left something out. Raksha, who raised Mowgli, Akela, and their pack. There were no wolves.

Feral, in today's world, basically means at home in open country. That and some version of introverted, reticent, or simply different. My husband, Baloo, proficient in down-home, authentic small talk, an honest man, a says-what-he-thinks man, who speaks with specificity and nuance, not in cliché, has told me plainly how strange I am. By accent, movement, the severity of my expressions, as visible as the way a dog's tail gives away emotion, or with horses, their ears. He has also valued my particular strangeness such that I have learned to also. This is why we need others who care about us in order to know ourselves. This is also why the lone wolf story is fabricated. Like wolves, we need our people to belong.

That night I slept in my childhood bedroom, remembering the old stained glass image of a howling wolf that once hung in the windowpane of the French doors that opened onto a small balcony. A gray wolf, head tipped skyward, with an indigo, violet, and turquoise colored mosaic night sky for background. Sunlight reflected through the colored glass framed in an oval of brass. As a girl, I stared into it often. It felt like a portal to another world. A world I continue to walk toward.

Language Born of Territory

I do not write because I trust words
or even because I like them

it is the softness in your eyes I look for
warmth, someone to count on

I do not write to persuade or justify
or tell you anything especially new

I write to navigate my way safely
across the chasm of words offered as bait

the old wolf must be wise enough
to sniff out poison, not die by strychnine

land mines
there is grief

and there is the curvature of grief
my shadow outlined on asphalt midsummer

I write because I distrust words
so much I've determined to do justice to them

this is how people hurt each other:
they say one thing, do another

then stare at you
like you're the incongruous one

when you twitch
when a tear falls

all the way down to your chin
words mobilize people to war

words are bullets are knives
are more unforgettable than scars

words: a gift of the gods
language: born of territory

how we speak, then act
the people we become
<><><><><><><><><>

TO DO VIOLENCE

The number of people reportedly killed by a wolf in North America since 1922 is six. Two by wild wolves. Two by captive wolves. And two because of being bitten by wolves who had rabies.[45]

When I searched figures on wolf-related deaths on Wikipedia, I found two cases since 2000. In 2005, a young man was killed by wolves who had been habituated to people's garbage in Points North Landing, Saskatchewan. A bush pilot had warned him that the wolves had become aggressive. And in 2010 a young woman out jogging near Chignik, Alaska, was found dead, mauled by wolves, but with circumstances unclear other than to "confirm wolf involvement."[46] Mosquitoes, though, have probably killed more people than any other creature, certainly more than any carnivore. And humans, of course, killing each other.

In the United States, domestic dogs kill 20 to 30 people each year.[47] Roughly another 20 people per year lose their life to incidents with cattle. To say that plainly, domestic dogs and cows kill far more people than wolves do, yearly.[48] Having grown up around longhorn

---

45   "List of Wolf Attacks in North America," Wikipedia, https://en.wikipedia.org/wiki/List_of_wolf_attacks_in_North_America.

46   "List of Wolf Attacks in North America."

47   Peterson, *Wolf Nation*.

48   Peterson.

cattle, I have a good deal of respect for the charging bull, or anxious mama cow who feels cornered, and am careful not to put myself in such a vulnerable position. I learned to herd the cows through walking. Slowly. That, and on horseback, which is certainly more effective across wide terrain. Four-wheelers are too noisy, but safer, I am told, when herding bison.

One time, a friend decided to take a walk from the old ranch house on my family's land to the big open bowl of a meadow up the creek, on the neighbor's side. He carried his trumpet with him, thinking how nice it would be to play a song out there amid the dusty grass and amphitheater of live oaks. About a half-hour later, he came back, short of breath from running, with a story. Said he'd started playing some trumpet tune and startled the neighbor's herd. He said they came at him, charging. Cows, it turns out, are more dangerous than wolves.

The Norwegian Institute for Nature Research led a report covering 400 years of recorded history in North America and Eurasia concerning wolf attacks on people. It writes that the episodes where wolves have preyed on people are scattered and often associated with an "evil spirit," indicating predatory wolf attacks are not normal. It puts it in plain terms: "The risks of being attacked by a wolf are not zero, but are clearly so low that they are virtually impossible to quantify, especially when compared to the other background risks associated with living."[49] I cannot help but evoke a

49 Norwegian Institute for Nature Research (NINA), *The Fear of Wolves: A Review of Wolfs Attacks on Humans*, A Large Carnivore Initiative for Europe (Trondheim, Norway: NINA, January 2002), http://www.nina.no/archive/nina/PppBasePdf/oppdragsmelding/731.pdf.

Norwegian accent in reading that, the matter-of-factness of it, which I find most refreshing.

American wildlife tracker and author David Moskowitz writes in *Wolves in the Land of Salmon* about tracking wolves across a couple of days and on return to his truck finding wolf scat and tracks right beside it, realizing he wasn't the one tracking so much as the one being tracked.[50]

While wolf attacks have been exceptionally rare in North America, there is a history of sporadic but clustered incidents of attacks in Europe and Asia, rabies accounting for most of these.[51] The word "rabies" comes from the Sanskrit word *rabhar*, "to do violence."[52] It is a viral infection of the nervous system. Wolves do not serve as a reservoir for the disease but are susceptible to spillover from domestic dogs and jackals, as well as Arctic foxes in the North. Many rabies attacks attributed to wolves have also actually been by feral dogs or wolf-dog hybrids, just as attacks by domestic dogs (rabid or not) are far more common than attacks by wolves. Rabid dogs have likely killed many more people than rabid wolves.[53] Still, here we have a virus projected onto an animal, one animal in particular.

Brett Walker, author of *The Lost Wolves of Japan*, reflects how "in Ainu stories, a sense of admiration for animals is revealed; in Japanese stories, a sense of anxiety."[54] The reason for that anxiety could be understood as rooted in the agrarian lifeway that had separated people from the mountains, depicted through "the deities *ta no*

---

50   Moskowitz, *Wolves in the Land of Salmon*.
51   Moskowitz.
52   NINA, *The Fear of Wolves*.
53   NINA.
54   Walker, *The Lost Wolves of Japan*, 95.

kami (paddy diety) and *yama no kami* (mountain deity)," differentiating between the "this world" of settled agricultural villages and the "other world" of the mountains, where the Ainu continued to live. But then came rabies, "which transformed the wolf from a benign creature to a deadly one."[55] Mad wolves, human-killers. Before the 1730s, people had never heard of "mad dogs" biting people in eastern Japan, but when rabies reached Japan from Korea and China, everything changed.[56] "With the demon rabies burning red hot in the brain of the large-Mouthed Pure God, the wolf became a monster of sorts, and ceremonial hunts, events that might be seen as forms of otherworldly exorcisms, focused on cleansing the mountains of the demon wolf."[57] The other sweeping change that would define people's perception of wolves was the force of industrialization.

The earliest wolf bounties in Japan date back to the early 17th century, mostly because of horse depredation.[58] In the mid-1700s, Japanese physician Negishi Yasumori, familiar with the drug strychnine, used it as a poison concealed in raw salt to assist ranchers in protecting their horses from wolves.[59] Dynamite was another method. Strychnine did not become widespread in Japan until after the Meiji Restoration of 1868, when a bounty system was put in place for wolves, as well as bears, ravens, and crows. Killing off wolves led to killing anything in the mountains, and a slow but stalwart change in perception of nature and all that exists outside the realm of human control.

55 Walker, 98.
56 Walker.
57 Walker, 118.
58 Walker.
59 Walker.

After two and a half centuries of samurai rule, the Tokugawa shogunate fell to, what is called by historians, the Satchō alliance. A political and military alliance between a handful of feudal domains. The Meiji Restoration. Over the next few decades, this alliance would replace Japan's decentralized early modern polity with a centralized modern one, taking notes from abroad. The Meiji government's pledge: end isolation from Western countries. "For a time, knowledge was indeed actively sought throughout the entire world: Japanese wrote a Prussian-style constitution, built an English-style navy, and established an American-style agricultural college on Hokkaido." One key advisor in the arena of "modern agriculture" and "scientific ranching" was none other than Ohio rancher Edwin Dun.[60]

As part of the colonization of Hokkaido, the Meiji government promoted ranching. Dun thus overtook the task of eliminating wild dogs and wolves from southeastern Hokkaido. He would draw on his own experience in the Midwest to lace bait with strychnine in the kind of unfathomable quantities once spread across North America.[61] "Poisoning wolves was no longer a 'strange way' to kill them but an example of industrial efficiency."[62]

American poet CAConrad, who describes themself as "the son of white trash asphyxiation whose childhood included selling cut flowers along the highway for his mother and helping her shoplift," has offered this apt summary: "efficiency breeds brutality."[63] Efficiency

60   Walker, 129.
61   Walker.
62   Walker, 138.
63   Jonathan Hobratsch, "2017 Poetry Month: An Interview with CA Conrad," *Huffpost*, April 21, 2017, http://www.huffingtonpost.com/entry/2017-poetry-month-an-interview-with-caconrad_us_58de83b5e4b0ca889ba1a53c.

that justifies homogenization, industrial profiteering, a silencing of the world.

It was under the Meiji government when the wolf earned the reputation of a "noxious" animal, daring to cut into their bottom line of industrial ranching. "With striking ease, Meiji officials brushed aside centuries of reverence for and fear of wolves – and, to a lesser degree, the entire East Asian order that supported such traditions – replacing them, brick by brick, with the edifice of a modern order."[64] Many Ainu, whose hunting and fishing lifeways were lost in the wave of forced assimilation that swept Hokkaido after 1800, reluctantly became professional hunters for hire, forced not only to kill wolves but also deer for the venison canneries that opened up, devastating the deer population.[65]

Hokkaido's deer population plummeted in 1878–1879, leaving wolves little option but to hunt domestic animals, namely horses. Because horse breeding had become big business, the situation was serious. Dun sent to Tokyo and Yokohama for all the strychnine to be had, and then, fearing there was not enough, he sent a supplementary order to San Francisco for more. In the end, Dun concluded, "We succeeded in getting enough to poison every living thing on the island."[66] In one generation of Meiji Japanese, wolves were erased from the Japanese archipelago.[67]

By the turn of the century, the Ashio copper mine, whose wealthy owners the Meiji government supported unconditionally, had created

64 Walker, *The Lost Wolves of Japan*, 133.
65 Walker.
66 Walker, *The Lost Wolves of Japan*, 152.
67 Walker.

Japan's first major pollution disaster. The inevitable result of living as if nature were inanimate: polluted waters, contaminated lands, sacrifice zones, sacrificed lives. Somehow I cannot separate strychnine to kill wolves imported from San Francisco under the watch of an Ohio rancher from the mining that followed. The disasters are paired here as elsewhere. Cull and then dig. The interests of a few justifying, well, anything. Walker reflects how Japan came to reflect other modern industrialized nations "almost more than it resembled its own premodern self."[68] Somewhat like the United States, Japan had come to resemble a "Neo-European landscape."[69]

Anyone who investigates wolves comes around to this type of reflection, what it is that wolves – and the destruction or manipulation of them – shows us about ourselves, how we have come to live, and what we have lost in getting there.

While 1905 is held up as the extinction date for wolves in Japan, some people (riffing off stories told by old woodcutters) argue that wolf extinction actually occurred in the aftermath of the Pacific War, when Japan's industrial recovery led to massive deforestation. So it could very well be that the forges of war, requiring an industrial lumber industry, not hunters or even rabies, killed off the last wolves of Japan sometime after 1945.[70]

Silence.

68   Walker, 157.
69   Walker, 166.
70   Walker.

Echo: freight train thunder

    corpses
        songs to remember by

MIS/UNDERSTANDING WOLF

The closest I have been in real proximity to wolves is following tracks in wet mud and hearing that eerily beautiful wolf howl late at night over a campfire on my 23rd birthday, just across the Canadian border from Southeast Alaska en route to Mount Edziza. I was leading a group of Alaskan "troubled youth" on a seven-week immersion in the backcountry, as much healing for me as I hope it was for them. Canoeing the Stikine River and walking our way toward this volcanic peak known for its obsidian in the Tahltan Highland, whose territory we were in. It was a calm night, no rain, and I stayed up tending the fire with my colleagues on a rocky knoll overlooking thick forest. We only heard wolves that night.

I've seen more wolves contained. A lone Idaho pair caged for show in the Black Hills, South Dakota. In Ely, Minnesota, where I saw a pack of gray wolves through a glass pane curled up in soft dirt. Another pack of dusty-white wolves roaming around their enclosure at the Grizzly & Wolf Discovery Center in West Yellowstone, Montana. And Mexican gray wolves at the Living Desert and San Francisco zoos. Though there was also the lone collared gray wolf I glimpsed while driving a northern Michigan highway, standing watchful on a high berm at the edge of the treeline.

The first time I saw a pasty old American man wearing a "SEE A WOLF KILL A WOLF" T-shirt was in Moscow, Russia, in front of a cafe with the only available menus written in Cyrillic. I was listening to him loudly and with impressive self-righteousness demand a menu in English: "For fuck's sake. Terrible service." I wanted to shoot him.

There are two crucial things that happen to Wolf. Wolf is romanticized. Wolf is hated. When really wolves are being objectified and thoroughly misunderstood. In the ironic words of US federal agent, Bert Hegewa: "They're just the knowin'est brutes on four legs, sometimes they're almost human."[71]

The associations are many and diametrically varied. Wolf as scapegoat, villain, outcast. Wolf as warrior, guide, mother to stray or orphaned children, as well as her own pups. A wolf mother figures in the legend of the founding of Rome.

Romulus and Remus, twin sons of a Vestal Virgin, Mars the supposed father. At birth they are banished. Abandoned to a cave known as the Lupercal, said to be located at the southwest foot of the Palatine Hill in Rome. A she-wolf nurses the twins here until a swineherd named Faustulus finds them and decides to take them home. His wife was rumored to be a lupa, prostitute or she-wolf (you pick, the word means both). The twins are raised by wolves. They become the founders of Rome.[72] There are two elements to this story: the she-wolf who nursed the twins when they were abandoned, and then Faustulus's wife, the lupa.

71   Walker, *The Lost Wolves of Japan*, 176.
72   Lopez, *Of Wolves and Men*.

The *Capitoline Wolf* sculpture of the she-wolf suckling the twins has been a symbol in Rome since ancient times. Similarly, in Greek mythology, Leto, mother of the twins Artemis and Apollo, is reported to have given birth to them as a she-wolf to evade Hera.

There are many stories about Wolf as guide. The Hirpini People of Italy, a place somewhat full of wolf symbolism, are said to have found their first home site because they were led there by a wolf. The Osco-Umbrian word for wolf is *hirpus*.[73]

Turkic legends also say people were descendants of wolves. Asena, an old Turkic story, tells of how the people were created. A small Turkic village is raided by Chinese soldiers, and one baby is left behind. An old she-wolf with a sky-blue mane named Asena finds the baby and nurses him, raising him as her own. She later gives birth to half-wolf, half-human cubs. Ancestors of the Turkic People.[74]

Wind Cave in the Black Hills, South Dakota, is the point of emergence for the Lakota People. The natural entrance is a breathing hole that, on low-pressure days, exhales air as strong as gusting wind. A signal of storms on the way. Maka Oniye in Lakota, "breathing earth." I have stood there many times, picking wild currants and feeling the stone cold cavern air wash over me on a hot summer day. The breathing hole so impressed upon my 3-year-old son that he became convinced this is the place where the thunderstorms live. Wilmer Mesteth, tribal historian from the Cheyenne Creek community on the Pine Ridge Indian Reservation of the Oglala Lakota Tribe, described how the cave's entrance has shrunk in size, nowadays

73 "European Kingdoms: Ancient Italian Peninsula," The History Files, https://www.historyfiles.co.uk/KingListsEurope/ItalyHirpini.htm.
74 "Asena," Wikipedia, https://en.wikipedia.org/wiki/Asena.

impassable, a reminder of origin. While there are different versions of the Lakota emergence story, Mesteth told of one in which Wolf, together with Iktomi, Spider, guided the people to the surface. Wolf: Sungmanitu Tanka.[75] *Tanka* means great. Similar to the word for bison, Tatanka, who is considered a gift from the Creator.

The Kiowa have a story about the red wolf, Gui-Goodle-Tay, who taught them the songs of the Gourd Dance, Tdie-pei-gah, meaning "ready to go, ready to die." It is a man's dance, a warrior dance. The story goes that when the Kiowa People still lived around the Black Hills, and what is known as Devils Tower, or otherwise Bear Lodge, a Kiowa warrior was separated from the main camp and, after traveling many days, became weak from hunger. Nearing exhaustion, he heard someone singing in the distance. He followed the sound to the top of a hill, and on the other side stood a red wolf on his hind legs, singing one beautiful song after another. At the end of each song, the red wolf would give a strong howl. The man listened, entranced. Then, with dusk approaching, the red wolf invited him to come down for some food and water. After regaining his strength, he listened to the instructions of the wolf, who had saved him from death, instructions that told the warrior to take the song and dance back as a gift to his people. This would become the Gourd Dance.

In the late 1880s, the federal government forbid the Kiowa, as well as all Plains tribes, to practice their ceremonial dances. The Gourd Dance continued, but underground. In 1955, a group of Kiowa men who remembered some of the songs and the dance revived the Kiowa Gourd Dance officially. Two years later, it was

75   "The Lakota Emergence Story," Wind Cave National Park, https://www.nps. gov/wica/learn/historyculture/the-lakota-emergence-story.htm.

formally recognized and spread across the Nation. Today, it is a yearly celebration. At the end of all Gourd Dance songs, the wolf must be paid tribute through a howl.[76]

The story of wolf girls Amala and Kamala is well documented, with black and white photos and a missionary's diary from the early 1920s. Two sisters deserted by their mother and adopted by a wolf mother, later found in the forest by Reverend J.A.L. Singh, were taken to an orphanage in Midnapore, India, to be broken like wild mustangs. In a cross-genre book of poetry, Bhanu Kapil writes lucidly about these feral daughters raised as wolves, and the brutality of the man who wanted to force them back into being properly human. They both died within a few years of being held captive.

From *Humanimal*, by Bhanu Kapil:

27. A woman left her daughters beneath a tree then tiptoes back to town. A wolf woke up deep in the tree. A girl was a speck on the ground, so the wolf picked her up in her hairy beak and flew off into the trees. When the girl was found in a milky cave, they shot her mother the wolf and tore her out of her hair. Then there was tea. Sugary tea with milk sucked from a rag, and they bound her pelvis in cotton. There is a formal photograph that survives in anthologies of this period: the wolfgirl seated, center front of a row of orphans at Joseph's feet. The eyes of the good children do not waver. When the photographer shouts from under his black cape – 1, 2, 3 – our

76   "The Story of the Red Wolf/The Gourd Dance: Kiowa Culture," YouTube, https://www.youtube.com/watch?v=LRBFLwf5CK8.

girl is the only one who looks up at a raven passing overhead, shaking her head like a dog on a rope, to howl. "Owowwoow." Joseph kicks her hard, his face completely blank for the camera, but it is too late. It is 1924. The photograph will be blurry. Two faces blossom from one neck.[77]

Another common association is Wolf as danger, a predatory man. One of the first fearful characters many engage with as children is the false wolf: Big Bad. Take the image of the big bad wolf. Imagine it. Ghastly, leering, cartoonish. A shaggy brute with big teeth, salivating. A wolf, really? Or a predatory man? The Little Red Riding Hood fable itself can be seen as the suggestion of nature as evil. She goes into the forest and finds danger – personified by Wolf – there.

In France, Germany, and Slavic countries, Wolf has also been conceived as a corn spirit. When the wind sets the corn (rye) in wave-like motion, the old saying was "the wolf is going over, or through, the corn," "the rye-wolf is rushing over the field," or simply "the wolf is in the corn."[78] Children were warned about the corn-wolf or rye-wolf, who is not a common wolf but has the outward appearance of a wolf. In the days of East Prussia, it has been said that if peasants saw a wolf, they would watch to see how the wolf carried her tail, in the air or dragging along the ground. If the latter, they would go after this wolf in thanks for blessing their fields, otherwise they would go hunting to kill.[79]

77 Bhanu Kapil, *Humanimal: A Project for Future Children* (Berkeley, CA: Kelsey Street Press, 2009), 32.

78 Sir James George Frazer, *The Golden Bough* (New York: Macmillan Publishing, 1922), 519.

79 Frazer.

In Saudia Arabia, there are two plants named after wolves: *Awshaz*, a tree with large thorns and small red berries, which the Badu People call "wolves' blood." And *ghada*, a small bush with long-burning wood known to keep people warm on cold desert nights, which desert poets of pre-Islamic Arabia apparently referred to by calling the wolf "master of the ghada."[80]

Then we have wolf as werewolf, made up. Medieval Europe, the Roman Catholic Church. Werewolves were an idea, a propaganda tool. During this heyday of the Holy Inquisition, the Church proclaimed people werewolves to justify killing anyone deemed a threat to their agenda of control. People exploiting the image of wolves to evoke fear, wolf became devil. Then that same fear and hatred was associated with the werewolf. Human-wolf. Human who embodies qualities of the wolf: midwives, herbalists, so-called pagans. Kill them, kill them all. These were barbaric centuries. Deepening fears about the wolf over and over again. Deepening fears about wolf-like wisdom. How to live through instinctive knowing and not just bow down to the rules dictated by a regime.

Stories of werewolves led to mass killings. Such as when "a single French magistrate between 1598 and 1600 sentenced to death six hundred citizens accused of being werewolves."[81] There is a generic awareness of this era in Europe when witches were murdered, when the Church went after pagans (nonbelievers) with a vengeance, when healers were burned at the stake. This happened, but what gets overlooked is how it was associated with Wolf.

80   Yousef Al-Mohaimeed, *Wolves of the Crescent Moon* (New York: Penguin Books, 2003), 176–177.
81   Moskowitz, *Wolves in the Land of Salmon*, 239.

Lobotomize

call anguish hysteric
of the womb / of the wolf den
so that pain isn't registered
as something to feel
the weight of the gun in hand
she's just a crazy
just a wild and dangerous

where are your people from?
why did they come here?

white walls blank cut paper
starched cotton coarse against
bare skin don't forget why
(y/our) people came here:
starvation war razed memories
lead poison aristocratic thievery
healers burned old growth lit
flames extinguished . extinct

stop trying to control what you don't
understand – stop –

wolf hunt witch hunt wolf hunt
witch hunt wolf hunt which hunt?
the forest breathes softly

snowflakes cushion sound
old cedar wears raven
for a headdress
until raven caws
soars aloft
follows wolves
to the clearing
blood red blue ice
a dead moose
whose antlers rest
on wet snow
||<>|<>|<>||

WOLF IS ANOTHER
WORD FOR WOMAN

The *Hammer of Witches*, the handbook of the Inquisition, explains that the sorcerer can bewitch "by a mere look or glance from the eyes," which could account for the origins of the French idiom *elle a vu le loup*, "she's seen the wolf," insinuating she's lost her virginity.[82]

The Hammer of Witches also reads verbatim: "No one does more harm to the Catholic church than do the midwives."[83] Ever since reading that single line, I cannot shake it from my memory. In a terribly frightening way, it says it all.

To say, "I gave birth" in Spanish is *di a luz*. Literally: I gave light. In Danish, the word for midwife is *jordmor*, earth mother. In Icelandic, it is *ljósmóðir*: mother of light. The Mohawk word is *iewirokwas*: "she's pulling the baby out of the Earth."[84] Katsi Cook, Mohawk midwife, is quoted often for this beautiful synthesis: "Woman is the first

---

82   Lopez, *Of Wolves and Men*, 219.

83   Elizabeth Davis, *Heart & Hands: A Midwife's Guide to Pregnancy & Birth*, 4th ed. (Berkeley, CA: Celestial Arts, 2004), 1.

84   Katsi Cook, "Cook: Women Are the First Environment," Indian Country Today, December 23, 2003, https://indiancountrytoday.com/uncategorized/cook-women-are-the-first-environment#:~:text=In%20the%20Mohawk%20language%2C%20one,bodies%20are%20the%20same%20water.

environment. In pregnancy our bodies sustain life. At the breast of women, the generations are nourished. From the bodies of women flows the relationship of those generations both to society and the natural world. In this way the earth is our mother, the old people said in this way we as women are earth."[85] Women are born with all our eggs. This means memory is carried differently. Wolves are the only animals I am aware of who are attributed with mothering humans.

Kill the wolves and the land suffers. Kill the midwives and the women and children suffer. Associate the two and create deep divisions in people's psyches that for generations will not lose hold: wolf as demon, woman as trouble. Both of which must be subdued. In Mexico, Fray Ruiz de Alarcón began his Inquisitorial report to the Holy Office by addressing birth as "the ritual that will bring 'clarity' to the Spanish about Indigenous 'heathen' beliefs."[86] Notice who gets called heathen. Notice the convenience of this word.

The Holy Inquisition demonized midwives as werewolves. Herein was the beginning of men taking the role of "earth mother" – as an industry – an industry contemptuous of innate knowledge/in*born* knowing. That adrenaline (stress) opposes oxytocin, that oxytocin is a love hormone, that mothers do not bond well if their babies are taken away from them, that animals will reject their young if bonding is not allowed, that we are animals, that Pitocin, epidurals, and other interventions inhibit theta brain waves to prevent the hormonal elixir, that the body goes instinctive during birth, that we

---

85 "Tekatsi:tsia'kwa Katsi Cook," Indspire, 2016, https://indspire.ca/laureate/sherrill-katsi-cook-barreiro/.

86 Patrisia Gonzales, *Red Medicine: Traditional Indigenous Rites of Birthing and Healing* (Tucson: The University of Arizona Press, 2012), 74.

must trust ourselves completely, that birth is not a medical activity, a matter of convenience, a pharmaceutical tycoon's source of profit, that breast milk is sustenance is medicine is requisite, that touch is sustenance is medicine is requisite, that this dismissal is intended, is not ignorance, is calculated. Where there is love there is no question.

European misinterpretations of cultures different from their own were characterized by imposed constructs of inferiority. Dualism, a refracting of vision. Concepts of witches, devils, and wild women were introduced while colonials interrogated Indigenous People in search of the tall tales they'd carried with them on those creaky schooners across the sea. Scholars of this content put it simply: European men feared women could control them.[87] Fray Andrés de Olmo's 1553 book of sermons against witchcraft includes a section on why the devil ministers more to women than men. De Olmos claimed the devil as the teacher of midwives.[88] Wolf is also associated with the devil.

In *Red Medicine: Traditional Indigenous Rites of Birthing and Healing*, Patrisia Gonzales, granddaughter of Kickapoo, Comanche, and Macehual peoples, writes:

The Inquisition and colonial authorities utilized public displays of power to repress Indigenous worldview and replace the grand pre-Columbian public ceremonies. Public trials replaced the feasts where the ticitl and the temixihuitiani (someone who causes to give birth, midwife) or the tepalehuiani (helper or midwife) once danced with bunches of marigolds and

87 Gonzales, *Red Medicine*.
88 Gonzales.

tobacco in honor of Tlazolteotl, the guardian of midwives, medicine and birth.[89]

Nature, from Latin *nātūra*, means quality, substance, essence. The feminine form of *nātūrus*, future active participle of *nāscor, gnāscor*: to be born.[90] For every human born, there is the initial association with the mother, and then there is the association with the world we inhabit. The initial association, with mother, has been repeatedly violated by excessive techno-medicalization, birth interrupted, babies forcibly separated from their mothers after unnecessarily manipulated births. An emphasis on efficiency, on mechanical predictability, on profitable convenience.

The criticism of overmedicalized birth is a critique of control as an excuse to profit, conditions that do not cater toward a woman's biological sense of safety, a forcefulness of unnecessary interventions, florescent hospital lights, random people examining at random times, being forced to lie down so instruments are attached to machines for liability purposes, cutting women open when there is no real emergency, for which the statistics are shockingly disproportionate. The majority of hospital procedures are factually more informed by acquiring legally defensible documentation than facilitating natural birth.[91] Countries with the lowest infant mortality rates use midwives as primary care providers for healthy, low-risk

89 Gonzales, 77.
90 Richard Louv, *Last Child in the Woods: Saving Our Children from Nature-Deficit Disorder* (Chapel Hill, NC: Algonquin Books of Chapel Hill, 2005).
91 Elizabeth Davis and Debra Pascali-Bonaro, *Orgasmic Birth: Your Guide to a Safe, Satisfying and Pleasurable Birth Experience* (Emmaus, PA: Rodale Books, 2010).

women. All the while the art of midwifery has been made illegal, midwives forced underground, factually persecuted, like wolves.

From the [un]Holy Inquisition to the 1950s era post-war madness, unprecedented loss became of global occurrence. World War II is markedly the point on the chart with the most pronounced spike in accounting for exponential losses within the fabric of life. A spike paired precisely with the increase of toxic chemicals, plastics, nuclear waste, which also happens to be the same point in time when male doctors overrode the profession, tied women to the bed and gave them scopolamine, a drug to erase memory. When safety became associated strictly with hospitals, not homes, was also when all the leftover war chemicals were made into pesticides and fertilizers, sold to farmers at a premium. This spike on the charts of oblivion looks a lot like a stock sheet graph, bending upwards to this day.

It all ties back to industrialization, of course, colonialism as an economic scheme. Yet there is something more here, more than shepherds or cattlemen killing wolves because they lost some money, more than men wanting to control birth for profit. The association is evidenced in the way wolves, like women and midwives (or otherwise women and midwives, like wolves), have been projected upon. Made into a different version of themselves; made into something *problematic*, someone *difficult*.

When my health insurance rejected my request for out-of-network coverage to hire a home birth midwife (of which there are no options in the network), I wrote an appeal. After outlining the many ways in which home birth is safer (for women with no adverse health conditions), cheaper, more conducive to women staying in control of their own birth, and that considering pregnancy and birth are *natural physiological events*, my last line stated simply: "I am asking that you honor my request for safety and self-determination as a mother." Sylvia Ledesma, guardian of ceremonial knowledge of the Azteca Conchero tradition in the Xicano community, says it this way: "*Curandera de yo misma*," meaning curandera of myself. "Healing is part of our self-governance."[92]

After the inaugural parental bonds, the second association children forge is with the world around them. For most of human history, this took place in close contact with nature, amid unpolluted air and water, quite unlike the reality we experience today, in varying degrees of extremity, everywhere bending toward the ever more extreme, the ransacked. "In such a world there is no wildness, as there is no tameness," writes American author Paul Shepard in *Nature and Madness*.[93] A welcome confounding of the oft-assumed polarity. Today is a different matter. The obsession with control and dominion has taken a heavy toll; it has altered the world toward a fear-based drive for predictability, monotony, and bottomless economic appetite, in turn destroying beauty.

I read a story that took place in Turkey some years ago. People gathered to stand in the way of bulldozers aimed to raze 300-year-old trees in a favored city park, all because another corporate development was planned. People lost their eyes to tear gas for this. People died for this. People are being killed for loving places others have forgotten how to love, and people are making money by making places harder to love. Because to stand up for what you love

92   Gonzales, *Red Medicine*, 20.
93   Paul Shepard, *Nature and Madness* (Athens: University of Georgia Press, 1998), 8.

is a threat to the mediocrity of those in control. Control that begets fear, which begets forgetting what we know.

We have been told to forget, or never even know, that the word "wolf" translates to "guide," that midwifery translates to mother of earth, of light. That the fiction of werewolves was a way of hunting down healers, often women, often midwives, but also male healers, and this too is important to name. Because the attack is on knowledge, wolf-like knowing. So, against all the odds, we fight for "wildness" juxtaposed and "untamed" wisdom, which is actually a fight for self-determined beauty. The echo of wolves howling across the soft tundra when fireweed is blooming.

^^

Paw 1 size of a human palm. yet clawed, leather-soled with musculature. belonging to an intelligence unbridled. how to track caribou. hunt muskox. press heavy into the riverbank. leave wet muddy marks on the kitchen tent canvas. lunge. 2 tracks in red sand, four paw prints following your foot prints. you never even noticed. 3 I used to pride myself on the callouses over my foot soles. hardy pawed woman. barefoot trapeze artist climbing rim rock in the Pyrenees past a herd of geared-up hikers. 4 when Blixen, Rhodesian ridgeback, was a puppy, he tripped over the size of his own paws. he would grow into a dog who scared the shit out of people. that hefty sound of his bark. the width of his burgundy-amber paws with white cuffs. 5 I stare into the open palm of my own hand and imagine round padding, black claws, soft fur. a paw the size of my hand feels large. kindred. we really are so similar.

WOLF CULTURE

Wolf character: Familial. Animated. Curious. Playful. Devoted. More than any other canid, wolves are social animals. Full of expression.

Wolf language is complex; it is scent, movement, gesture, as well as sound. Biting another's nose is a sign of trust, care. Rolling, bending low, pulling ears back, these are all signals.[94] Wide eyes mean fear, narrowed eyes signify meanness. Prancing is a sign of play and surrender. Bending one's belly low to the ground and gazing with fondness is a show of submission, affection, even respect. Facial expressions, position of tail, ear, and head, all matter. That and ambrosia, the sweet scent of family, a scent wolves release from the gland on top of their tail, a scent of trust, marker of safety and home. Wolf packs will rub necks and chests over the scent glands on each other's tails to exchange odors, to join in one scent. Otherwise urine is used to mark territory.

Wolves have senses like psychics. With a single sniff a wolf can know if you are male or female, an adult or a child, hunting or not, if you are happy or sad. To pat the alpha wolf under the chin is a sure way of asking, gently, for friendship. To mouth another wolf on top

94   Jean Craighead George, *Julie of the Wolves* (New York: HarperCollins Publishers, 1972).

of the muzzle is to proclaim leadership of the pack. To roll on one's back is a show of surrender.[95]

If a human joins in a howl, wolves will change their pitch to harmonize with the person's voice.[96] There are different dialects and accents in their howling. This isn't unusual. A prairie dog's alarm call can encode the precise color and shape of the approaching threat. Humpback whales sing across hundreds of miles, signaling not just location but also identifying their particular family group.[97]

When trotting, wolves leave a single line of paw tracks, which is an advantage for efficient travel in deep snow or rough country. There is a Russian saying: "The wolf is fed by its feet."[98] They can run 35–40 miles per hour when pressed.[99] On average, wolves walk eight hours a day and can travel upwards of 75 kilometers per day, and again the next, and next. They eat animals sometimes ten times their size. They often starve.[100]

Wolves have 42 teeth, with the same general categories as our own. Canines, incisors, premolars.[101] Only they have about double as many teeth. They have big jaws. To pierce through the thick hair of a muskox, the hide of a moose, and clamp down while they kick and thrash.

Some are hunters of elk, others musk oxen, others still are wolves of the caribou. They create and maintain distinct cultures.

95   Craighead George.
96   Peterson, *Wolf Nation*.
97   Peterson.
98   Van Tighem, *The Homeward Wolf*, 14.
99   Savage, *Wolves*.
100 Huffman, *Medicine of the Wolf*.
101 Savage, *Wolves*.

Grasslands rely on wolves to choreograph herd movement, because without their orchestration the deer or elk get lazy, overgraze, and outnumber the land's capacity to renew. Overgrazing leads to erosion, then starvation. Wolves keep large herds in balance by harvesting the sick and infirm. They have babysitters, rituals, and spring and summer dens they might return to over generations. Some old Irish tales say that wolves who denned in caves were perceived as entering and exiting the other world.[102] The Irish word for wolf, *mac tír*, literally translates as "son of the earth."[103]

Wolves mate for life. They have lovers who, if one or the other is killed, will fight to avenge with reckless abandon. Their territories have periphery areas around pack boundaries, where their home territory overlaps with another wolf pack.

There is no visual distinction between night and day to wolves. They have light-gathering rods in their eyes that give them daytime vision at night.[104] It is said they can see right through you.

To account for the specifics of wolf language, character, intelligence is to appreciate particulars. The particulars of language, place, culture.

Denali National Park wolf researcher Dr. Gordon Haber was a scientist known to speak from direct experience, not computer formulated stats or myopic studies. A scientist who also gave his lived perspective and didn't limit it to engrained notions of what being objective means. He spent 43 years studying generations

102   Lenny Antonelli, "Lay of the Land: In the Ghost Wood," *Orion*, Spring 2021.

103   "'Wolf' in Different Languages."

104   Jean Craighead George, *Julie's Wolf Pack* (New York: HarperCollins Publishers, 1997).

of wolf families. His research findings included: wolves play on average every 30 minutes; their communication skills, like howling, are profound; and their social ties are "unsurpassed, even among humans." He knew wolves to travel hundreds of miles in order to return to their families, saw distinct personalities in each individual, and noticed their evidently complex emotional expressions. His conclusion: "Wolves can be considered a culture."[105]

By acknowledging wolves as complex, fascinating beings, he also asserted they cannot be managed by the simplistic models commonly used in wildlife management. Counting wolves over a particular area isn't enough to consider it a "healthy" population, because the "functional unit of wolves is the family, a multigenerational extended family group." He named the knowledge and experience of older wolves who know the territory, herd movements, hunting skills, den sites, and teaching and raising of pups – who, when killed, set off a chain of events that leave "most of the family group dead and the rest scattered, rag-tag orphans."[106] Speaking in this way meant he stood up in the face of anti-wolfers but also other wolf biologists who don't dare speak of animals akin to people.

His core message: "When it comes to wolves, it's not about numbers. It's about family. A wolf is a wolf when it's part of an intact, unexploited family group capable of astonishingly beautiful and complex cooperative behaviors and unique traditions." When allowed to live as wolves, traditions for hunting, pup rearing, and

105 Peterson, *Wolf Nation*, 35–36.
106 "Among Wolves: Gordon Haber's Insights into Alaska's Most Misunderstood Animal," Wolf Conservation Center, https://nywolf.org/2013/10/among-wolves-gordon-habers-insights-into-alaskas-most-misunderstood-animal/.

social behaviors, fine-tuned to a particular place, become unique to that family group, just like human cultures. He considered it to our benefit that wolves exist because their presence "evokes the sense of wonder that helps us not just to live, but to be alive."[107]

Denali wolves recognized Haber's bush plane, howling as Haber circled them, jotting down notes and taking photos. They wouldn't run from his plane, as they would others, the sharpshooters, the planes that came to kill if they wandered outside the park boundaries.[108]

In 2009, Haber crashed and died when his plane went up in fire. Two long-time Alaska residents heard him circling before noticing the eerie silence. Then they heard wolves howl. A death cry. A mourning song. They said they heard the wolves howl longer than they had ever heard wolves howl before.[109]

107   "Among Wolves."
108   Peterson, *Wolf Nation*.
109   Peterson.

Part of this indigenous lexicon is a belief that body refers to both the land and the beings who live upon it. They hold the same value. This is reflected in the Mojave or Makav language – the word for body is 'iimat and the word for land is 'amat. In conversation, each can be represented by the prefix mat-, meaning when one hears the word mat- used in conversation, one must know the context of the conversation in order to discern if the speakers are talking about the body of a person or the body of the land. One is injured as easily as the other. Both have memories. To take care of the earth is to take care of the self.

—NATALIE DIAZ, "A LEXICON OF THE INDIGENOUS BODY"

THE WORD FOR WOLF IS

I have found it impossible to write about wolves without writing about language, hence worldview and the manifold ways of comprehension that are embedded, assumed, burrowed into our minds, which shape how we think about and understand the world.

The Italian idiom, *bocca al lupo*, which is used in opera and theater to wish a performer good luck, literally translates as "into the wolf's mouth." The standard response is *crepi il lupo!* Meaning, "may the wolf die!" Or, more commonly, *crepi!* (may it die!).[110]

The Swedish and Norwegian term for wolf is *varg. Warg* in Old German, *verag* in Anglo-Saxon. The word means outlaw, bandit, or evil spirit. Those people banished from human society, exiled from the comforts of the village, and forced to live in the outskirts, in "the wild."[111] In this case, wild means alone. In this case, Wolf takes the blame for human behavior. The more common word today, as in Danish, is *ulv.* Simply, wolf. And all that we imagine that word to be.

I grew up between cultures. Cultures homogenous in the form of racial demographic, and also economically positioned, thanks to their particular colonial histories. The respective comforts of Danish socialism, and the unrequited gains of American capitalism.

110   "*In bocca al lupo*," Wikipedia, https://en.m.wikipedia.org/wiki/In_bocca_al_lupo.
111   NINA, *The Fear of Wolves*.

Yet cultures as different as the western edge of North America is to the seaside kingdom of Denmark. When I think of culture, I think first of land, season, topography. To my American family, I am the daughter of a Danish mother. To my Danish family, I am the daughter of an American man, a foreigner. To both I am kin, and yet kinship requires locality too.

This left me wandering in the space between borders. Neither fully from here nor there, traversing between places at once known and to which I am still foreign. A no [wo]man's land. In the desert, per se, a word people too often use associatively for empty and desolate. Overlooking the sweet water springs and maize fields. No, the desert is not an apt metaphor. I talked to my friend Lilian Hill about this misuse of the word "desert" once, on a walk on the edge of Flagstaff, Arizona, beneath the San Francisco peaks her people call Nuvatukya'ovi. She shook her head and sighed. The Hopi People grow maize and watermelons in the desert. They know where the springs are and where they are disappearing. The myriad of plants and animals who also call desert Home. Therefore, as a Hopi farmer herself, she knows Desert to mean something far more nuanced and familiar. I don't actually know what the correct metaphor is for spending my life traversing between places at once known and to which I am still foreign. I do know that I looked to the land I grew up on for a sure sense of belonging.

I couldn't fully speak to my Danish grandparents. They didn't know English, and I hardly spoke Danish. *Dansk*, my mother tongue that I never learned whole. There are other ways to communicate: gesture, humor, presence. My *morfar*, translated from Danish simply as "mother's father," was a farmer. His favorite things to do were to walk slowly through the dark forest with his wooden cane and swim in the Kattegat on the first day of summer, the water still pierced with winter cold. He smoked cigars, salted his food before tasting it, and had hands strong as leather. He played chess with us kids and always lost, smiling, teaching us how to win. He kept an artwork I made and gave him on the wall in his office. I remember that now. The particular texture of that watercolor. That and the blue entry door, the sound of tires on small white gravel stones, the creaky floorboards, the musty smell, the sour taste of red currants and gooseberries gathered from the bushes out back.

In the years after his passing, I have fond memories of drinking black coffee and smoking Prince cigarettes with *Mormor* on long midsummer days, her wearing an upturned rebels smile for the raw joy of getting her granddaughter to smoke with her. Denmark in the summer smells of wild roses and sea squalls. During World War II, when the Nazis invaded Denmark, she was forced to house and feed Nazi soldiers in her farmhouse. She ran messages to the underground resistance. I imagine her carrying handwritten notes pressed into the folds of white linen. She never spoke of it over those cigarettes and cups of coffee we shared. I learned about the past from other relatives.

Eventually, I learned enough Danish to get by after spending one long winter working as a bartender in Copenhagen and taking Danish classes. The teacher didn't quite know what to do with me. I had fine pronunciation and understood more than anyone else in the class, but my grammar and spelling were terrible. Years before, my first college English teacher in undergrad didn't know what to do with me either. She literally asked me if English was my second language because of the way I phrased things.

"The purveyance of knowledge is embedded in language,"[112] Okanagan author and scholar Jeannette Armstrong said to me once. She is a fluent speaker of her Syilx language. It's a single line that has run through my mind since. Knowledge in its different formations.

Metaphors common in the English language today cater to notions such as "bigger is better," an emphasis on dualism, and a tendency toward economic justification – embedded in patterns of speech. "Time is money" may be one of the most commonplace metaphors many abide by today, practically governing society.[113] Coupled with the metaphors "more is good" and "good is up," we have in summary the metaphorical concepts most deeply embedded into economic attitudes of consumerism and incessant growth.[114] Unquestioned. Animals are also referred to as "it," for which there is no such word in Ojibwe.[115]

When writing in English, I try to deconstruct certain habits and write/think from a more land-based worldview. I have considered how the unraveling of land-based worldviews happened in correlation with the abstraction of the alphabet. Letters, once symbols, replacing visual representations. Imagery turned into script. The abstract jargon of law and finance used with calculated purpose. Oral history dismissed so written words could be used in legal documents – sign here, any mark will do.

112 Jeannette Armstrong, personal communication with author, September 2019.
113 George Lakoff and Mark Johnson, *Metaphors We Live By* (Chicago: The University of Chicago Press, 1980).
114 Lakoff and Johnson.
115 Robin Kimmerer, "Speaking of Nature," *Orion*, March/April 2017, https://orionmagazine.org/article/speaking-of-nature/.

Determined to speak, and thus think, with more accurate metaphors, I have turned to Indigenous languages and lexicon for guidance, perspective, and inspiration. Ma'iingan. Languages still rooted in and responsible to place. How the Ojibwe tribes stand united in giving wolves safe haven on their territories.

At the Mokuola Honua language symposium in Hilo, Hawai'i, I listened to Nā'ālehu Anthony speak about Captain Cook and the missionaries and plantation owners who followed, imposing an entirely foreign construct of how to live. He said this: "The voice of our reflection shifted."[116] Language as reflection. Language as more than pronunciation and syntax. Language: an embodiment of histories and violence and memory. The Hawai'ian word for land is 'aina, which means more precisely "that which feeds or nourishes." Aloha 'aina for "sacred land." Aloha, a greeting. Also a lifeway.

Jassa is a Sámi word for a patch of snow "uncovered in late spring and covered up during winter." A patch of snow that allows a flock of reindeer to gather, to rest and cool off during the summer heat when the mosquitos are relentless. "Large enough to accommodate a flock of them and hard enough to withstand their daily grinding."[117] One word encompassing that much specificity.

Ticasuk, Inupiat, is a name meaning "where the four winds gather their treasures from all parts of the world...the greatest of which is knowledge."[118]

116   Nā'ālehu Anthony, speaking at the Mokuola Honua language symposium in Hilo, Hawai'i, September 2016.

117   Anniken Greve, Sámi Stories: Art and Identity of an Arctic People (Tromsø, Norway: Orkana akademisk, 2014), 71.

118   "Emily Ivanoff Brown," Notable People, University of Alaska, https://www.alaska.edu/uajourney/notable-people/nome/emily-ivanoff-brown/.

Yintah, Wet'suwet'en, means interconnectedness with all life. A worldview, a way of being. David de Wit, representing the Office of Wet'suwet'en, explained the word to me once in these terms: "All life for us include abiotic elements like mountains, rocks, air and water. The health of the people are a reflection of the health of the land."[119] For years, the Wet'suwet'en Yintah and the headwaters of the river Wedzin Kwa have been threatened by the TransCanada/ Coastal GasLink pipelines, in cahoots with the governments of British Columbia and Canada. Another pipeline. Under another river. Against the will of the people who live there, who have always lived there. We are living in a moment where Indigenous words for life are being raised up in the face of these last-gasp, extractive industry forces, demanding people choose where they stand. DAPL. Mni Wiconi. Line 3. Manoomin. CGL. Yintah.

As Hugh Brody, British author of *The Other Side of Eden*, has said perceptively: "The clearing of minds is inseparable from the securing of lands."[120] It makes it harder for the takers, it turns out, when minds are full of specific intergenerational place-based knowledge concerning relationship to a territory, and to the animals who dwell or return there. This, at least in part, is why Indigenous languages have been so ruthlessly targeted for erasure.

Years ago, I learned an Inuit word that means in an encompassing way: world, outdoors, weather and universe, as well as awareness and sense. I obsessed over this word, its embodied and external vastness,

119   David de Wit, personal communication with author, Office of Wet'suwet'en, Smithers, BC, April 2018.

120   Hugh Brody, *The Other Side of Eden: Hunters, Farmers, and the Shaping of the World* (New York: North Point Press, 2001), 210.

yet only recently did I locate the word itself – Sila – "arguably the most important concept in classic Inuit thought...occurring in senses that are intellectual, biological, psychological, environmental, locational, and geographical," in a sense a "super-concept, both immanent and transcendent in scope," as explained by Rachel Attituq Qitsualik.[121]

Papua New Guinea has a language count of over 850, making it the most linguistically diverse place on Earth.[122] It is also one of the most biodiverse. Rugged topography protected this place until recently. The usual suspects: mining, timber, oil, and gas. Today, machines invented by blitzkrieg minds to seabed mine, to mine the fucking sea floor, sit docked in the harbor, metals needed for "green" technology.

The night before he dies, an African gray parrot named Alex says to the human researcher who has spent 30 years studying him, "You be good, I love you."[123]

My grandfather tells his family he's going to die. Says they'd better come make their goodbyes. My mother flies to Denmark. People gather around the living room and share the whiskey she purchased in Duty Free. I'm not there, but I dream of him. I dream of kneeling in front of his old armchair and placing my hand in his, feeling his knobby, calloused farmer's hand enclose around mine. We speak. In Danish. And a few days later he dies.

121 "The Meaning of 'Sila,'" Talon Books, https://talonbooks.com/meta-talon/the-meaning-of-sila.

122 "Languages of Papua New Guinea," Wikipedia, https://en.m.wikipedia.org/wiki/Languages_of_Papua_New_Guinea.

123 Allora & Calzadilla, and Ted Chiang, "The Great Silence," e-flux Journal, Issue #65, May 2015, https://www.e-flux.com/journal/65/336684/the-great-silence/.

There are currently 3,700 endangered (human) languages in the world. That means there are 3,700 endangered ways of thinking, seeing, responding to the particulars of a given place. What do you prefer, monotony or tapestry? Silence or sounds you may not understand but which have layers upon layers of meaning for those who do.

Raven speak, wolf howl, horse dialect, prairie, Arapaho.

Isaac Macuna, Hee gua (one who cures the world), of the village Puerto Antonio along the banks of the Pirá Paraná River in the Northwest Colombian Amazon, was chanting in his maloca one night. I sat outside listening. His melodic tone passed through the palm-thatched walls like smoke. I asked my host Maximiliano García what the chant meant and if there was a message to its melody. He told me there is no translation but that it is an invocation of the old times, of the ancestors. I realized this liberated the chant, unbinding the sounds from the constraints of formal interpretation.

I once asked my friend Alejandro what the Quechua word for "expert" is, feeling annoyed with the common arrogance tied to it in the English language and seeking another perspective from another language, another worldview. "We call it *pacco*, meaning apprentice of a mountain, student of, where the mountain is the teacher."[124]

It makes economic sense to learn global rather than local languages. But languages aren't just ways of communicating, they are ways of thinking, different ways of seeing and understanding the world. Take, for example, the Lakota winter count, *waniyetu wowapi*. Years are described rather than given an exact number. The year the buffalo froze. The year the stars fell. A sophisticated and

124   Alejandro Argumedo, personal communication with author, February 2020.

detailed way of keeping record, albeit less rigid and more cyclical than numerical dates listed in accordance with wars, elections, and other hand-picked versions of events recorded by those who happened to have proprietary access to feather pens and parchment: December 29, 1890; June 25, 1876.

Kallalit Nunaat (White Earth), Greenland, adopted Kalaallisut as the official language in 2009, some 40 years after the rock band Sumé (meaning "where?") took to the streets singing only Kalaallisut in Copenhagen pubs. The band's lyrics criticized Danish colonial power. They were one of the major cultural catalysts for reclaiming this language born of the vast glacial homelands across Inuit territories in the High Arctic. Danish, in Greenland, is the colonial tongue, and yet for the Greenlanders I met there it was often more familiar to speak in Dansk than in English. Even through what was for all of us our second language, and across the old colonial divisions, there was a sense of affiliation that wouldn't have been if I only spoke in the other even more dominant colonial language I'm using to write this book.

Liisi Egede Hegelund and the kinship we shared, subtle yet distinct. I was the only one in the group staying at her hostel on the edge of Greenland's capital city Nuuk to speak Dansk. Also the only one with a child, a 5-month-old baby, who, that first night upon sitting around the communal dining table for lamb stew, she offered to hold with this simple statement: "I'll take the baby." Once in her arms, she walked straight off to the kitchen. I trusted her. I'd just met her. I sat there contentedly seeing him nestled against her black fur vest, Greenlandic baby language being cooed into his ears. At that time there was practically no one I would have let walk away with him. I am quite sure that remains the singular moment he was not in my or my husband's sight for well over the first year of his life.

I've always been in curious awe of intuition and have also respected it, learned to heed it. An English word for how trust and sense can guide knowing. I have noticed when and how people value this kind of sensory intelligence equally, or not, alongside other ways of knowing. Because intuition can defy the so-called rational. Hence, some welcome it, while others outlaw it. Make it varg, an outlawed wolf.

Liisi had a narwhal tusk on her wall, hanging straight rather than horizontally in between two windows facing the icy fjord. I noticed it, the tusk itself, but also how she'd placed it spiraling skyward. I told her as much, to which she smiled and spoke of her decision as a feminine one, a choice to place the narwhal tusk in a place that required perception; that was not on overt display. She gave me a pair of muskox moccasins for my son when we departed. The softest, warmest fur. I gave her a beeswax candle in the form of a lotus flower, the size of two palms cupped together.

Echo: star light

    broken glass
    knife blade

LEARNING THE
DESTRUCTIVE WAY

In a film from the mid '80s called *Arctic White Wolves in the Wild*, American wildlife photographer Jim Brandenburg and wolf biologist David Mech go to Ellesmere Island in northern Canada and live with a pack of snow-white wolves. In Inuit, Ellesmere Island is appropriately called Umingmak Nuna, "Land of Muskox,"[125] although Inuit People are not mentioned in this documentary.

Being on an island that far north, wolves' experience with humans had, at least at that time, been limited to Inuit People. They had little reason to fear people as wolves had learned to farther south. Therefore, the interactions between these two visitors and the wolf pack were straightforward. The wolves showed curiosity and, with time and growing familiarity, welcome and even trust.

Brandenburg and Mech camped a short walk away from a wolf den. During their time there, the alpha wounded his paw and couldn't hunt for a few weeks. So, the pack took care of him. Brandenburg describes watching this with awe. It went against everything he'd learned and come to expect. Survival of the fittest rhetoric. Live or

125   "Ellesmere Island," Wikipedia, https://en.wikipedia.org/wiki/Ellesmere_Island.

die. Here he witnessed what he'd assumed to be a uniquely human proclivity for taking care of one another when hurt or ill.

The day they packed up to board the airplane that had come to fetch them, Brandenburg, sad to be leaving, looked out the Plexiglas porthole window and saw the wolf pack sitting just beside the landing strip, as if to say goodbye.[126]

In 2011, federal protections for wolves in the United States were lifted, which in Minnesota was promptly followed by the opening of sport trapping and hunting seasons. Jim Brandenburg lives in northern Minnesota, and at this time had come to know some 19 wolves intimately, photographing them all, in particular the obsidian black alpha, leader of the pack, who had the biggest paws he'd ever seen. When the hunt opened, Brandenburg tried to talk down local hunters amid this mockery of hunting, but the black alpha wolf was killed. He even knew the man who killed him and threw his radio-collar off near the town of Ely. Brandenburg, an avid photographer all his life, stopped taking photos. Grief hit him like a freight train. "It broke my heart, it really destroyed me in some sense. I have not been the same."[127]

Writing about this very issue, Robert Shimek states, "Here in Minnesota, the major contention is the statewide wolf hunt that refuses to acknowledge the territorial jurisdiction of the tribes and the importance of a healthy relationship between Ma'iinganag and

126 "Video: Arctic White Wolves in the Wild," White Wolf Pack, http://www.whitewolfpack.com/2011/03/video-arctic-white-wolves-in-wild.html.

127 Ron Meador, "New Film Looks at Minnesota Wolf Hunt with the Freshness of an Outsider's Eye," MinnPost, April 10, 2015, https://www.minnpost.com/earth-journal/2015/04/new-film-looks-minnesota-wolf-hunt-freshness-outsiders-eye/.

Anishinaabeg." He aptly describes how Euro-American views consider wolves a "renewable resource," those deadpan and oft-used words, a "resource" that can be killed indiscriminately with "no significant social, cultural or political impact."[128] The impact is a heavy one, on wolf culture as well as Anishinaabe. Shimek speaks directly to the limits of a mind that names life in terms of numbers, not relationship.

In *The Breath of a Whale*, author Leigh Calvez writes about stopping, in her case being a practicing scientist, when she realized the Navy was downright lying about the detrimental effects of LFA sonar on whales.[129] I have often considered this: Does it really do service to amputate emotion in order to be a "good scientist," or an otherwise "rational person" in this world? It doesn't seem so.

American environmentalist Aldo Leopold, once a wolf hunter, became the nature writer and environmental advocate he is known as the day he met the eyes of a mother wolf dying:

My own conviction on this score dates from the day I saw a wolf die. We were eating lunch on a high rimrock, at the foot of which a turbulent river elbowed its way. We saw what we thought was a doe fording the torrent, her breast awash in white water. When she climbed the bank toward us and shook out her tail, we realized our error: it was a wolf. A half-dozen others, evidently grown pups, sprang from the willows and

128 Robert Shimek, "The Wolf Is My Brother: The Cultural, Spiritual, and Historic Relationship between Ojibwe Anishinaabe and Ma'iingan of the Great Lakes Region of North America," Binaakwii Giizis (Moon of the Falling Leaves), October 2013, https://www.scribd.com/document/254829826/The-Wolf-Ma-iingan-is-My-Brother#.

129 Leigh Calvez, *The Breath of a Whale* (Seattle: Sasquatch Books, 2019).

all joined in a welcoming melee of wagging tails and playful maulings. What was literally a pile of wolves writhed and tumbled in the center of an open flat at the foot of our rimrock.

In those days we had never heard of passing up a chance to kill a wolf. In a second we were pumping lead into the pack, but with more excitement than accuracy: how to aim a steep downhill shot is always confusing. When our rifles were empty, the old wolf was down, and a pup was dragging a leg into impassable slide-rocks.

We reached the old wolf in time to watch a fierce green fire dying in her eyes. I realized then, and have known ever since, that there was something new to me in those eyes – something known only to her and to the mountain. I was young then, and full of trigger-itch; I thought that because fewer wolves meant more deer, that no wolves would mean hunters' paradise. But after seeing the green fire die, I sensed that neither the wolf nor the mountain agreed with such a view.[130]

Leopold came to this knowledge the hard way, the destructive way, but he learned, and he began to embody a different guiding metaphor than Wolf as vermin. Herein was his transition from a need-to-control/cull mentality to an embodiment of something rooted more deeply in the land.

Beside a woodstove fire one fog-drenched night, I sat visiting with my friend Itoah Scott-Enns, in town from Yellowknife, Northwest Territories, when our conversation landed on wolves. Facing the

---

130   Aldo Leopold, *A Sand County Almanac* (London: Oxford University Press, 1949), 129–130.

glow of nectarine flames coursing through a sooty pane of glass, she looked up and reflected, "In my Tłįchǫ First Nation it is understood that one never wears wolf fur on their head, that's just too powerful. I've only ever seen wolf fur mitts once. Otherwise I can't say I've seen people ever use the fur of wolf for clothing. Rabbit, beaver, these are all common, but not wolf."[131]

We'd been talking about polar bears and how they're getting hungry. Hungry and mad. A friend of hers from Nunavut said the bears are angry at people for what we've done to the world, and they are showing it by smashing down people's hunting shacks, something they've never done before. Ellesmere Island wolves are getting aggressive too, Itoah mentioned, referring to the experience of another friend who works as an Arctic guide and said that, on his most recent trip to Ellesmere, his crew had to shoot at the pack surrounding them, never letting up, to get them to go away. Hungry, and maybe angry. Uncanny behavior in an uncanny time. A different scene to that which Brandenburg and Mech experienced some 30 years prior. The pace of changes in recent decades, more lately in mere years, accelerating. Ice sheets melting, fast. With a sigh of frustration, Itoah talked about how people give in to the opinion they should hunt wolves to try and protect the declining caribou herds. Caribou management plans in effect, where wolves are targeted, not the diamond mines gutting the land.

Across the Pacific Northwest, estimates figure there to be as few as 40 caribou still trekking back and forth across the borders between British Columbia, Idaho, and Washington, where decline

---

131   Itoah Scott-Enns, personal communication with author, October 2016.

started with industrial logging, removing crucial winter habitat. Caribou depend on large tracts of forests at both low and high elevations. Cutting down huge swaths of forest forced caribou into smaller and more concentrated areas, further depleting food sources. Industrial logging operations are especially ruinous at high elevations, where it takes decades for trees to even begin to establish again, and where the lichen, on which caribou depend, won't start growing until tree stands are at least 100 years old. Where power lines cross the land, often to connect industrial mining camps to electric grids, caribou, as well as reindeer, migration routes are obstructed, because to their eyes, which can perceive the ultraviolet spectrum, power lines appear to drip with lightning. Often wolves are blamed for loss of caribou instead of industry. Take the mining exploration helicopters, buzzing around relentlessly in search of ore. The rampant noise of these pursuers scatters the moose and the wolves, bringing wolves into other pack territories, causing confusion. Another one of the many disturbances unaccounted for by the mining industry.

Ironically, the largest global conservation NGOs supposedly working to "save" nature for the wolves, caribou, blue whale, and other iconic animals who photograph so well – Bengal tiger, snow leopard, giant panda – receive much of their funding directly from extractive industries, mining, oil, industrial agribusiness, and the like, or their stockholders, nicely referred to as "donors."

The plethora of plants, animals, seeds, insects, and languages has been on a steep and mounting decline. On the heels of the incomprehensible losses wrought by colonialism, of course, and yet more of the substance of life has been converted into money in a single generation than ever before in history. Since World War II. Since the atomic bomb. Chart loss of life, and notice as much. And at an ever more wicked clip in recent years.

Amid this perpetual loss of the past 50-odd-year window is when the Big Greens emerged. The same statistics they quote to this day – "Since 1970, global wildlife populations have suffered an average two-thirds decline"[132] – have taken place in the duration of their existence. They, who have had all the funding, plus a solid five decades or more of proving ground, have failed where they have led with the same mindsets that have destroyed the world. This may be different with regional staff, but the revolving door with big industry remains (and has not been denounced), and the discrepancy of funding commanded by Big Greens, instead of going to, say, Indigenous and local communities or organizations, is stark.[133] Made more stark, more painfully ironic, when one considers the significant fact that the vast majority of the world's remaining intact nature, in other words *biodiversity*, is on Indigenous lands.[134] Slowly realizing that the top-down narratives of colonized

132 "Draft UN Biodiversity Plan Risks Another Lost Decade for Nature," World Wildlife Fund, January 18, 2020, https://wwf.panda.org/wwf_news/press_releases/?1246866/Draft-UN-biodiversity-plan-risks-another-lost-decade-for-nature.

133 Michael Roberts, "Indigenous Communities Are Once Again Paying As Conservation Groups Continue To Get Paid," Green2.0, https://diversegreen.org/first-nations-development-institute-michael-roberts-indigenous-communities-are-once-again-paying-as-conservation-groups-continue-to-get-paid/.

134 John C. Cannon, "Indigenous Lands Hold 36% or More of Remaining Intact Forest Landscapes," Mongabay, January 16, 2020, https://news.mongabay.com/2020/01/indigenous-lands-hold-36-or-more-of-remaining-intact-forest-landscapes/.

wilderness are blatantly incorrect (or simply giving in to mounting criticism and exposés), these aristocrats have smartened up to their misgivings. Not necessarily in order to change their institutions, but to make carbon markets sound like an Indigenous "partnership."

The carbon market is an economic scheme premised on offsetting carbon emissions. Favored by multinational corporations because offsetting does not actually require extraction or pollution to cease. A recent in-depth investigation by the *Guardian* revealed that over 90 percent of all so-called rainforest offsets, by the biggest certifier thereof, are worthless in terms of actually sequestering carbon or protecting forests.[135] Even of the projects that were deemed to protect standing forests there are other issues: violent land grabs from the communities who live there, who have protected the forests all along.[136]

So, today, instead of thriving caribou herds and wolf packs managed through local intergenerational knowledge, we still have unfettered extraction and so-called protected areas, many of which have the known reputation for kicking people off their homelands while still allowing industrial extraction within these very border zones.[137] And now, instead of harnessed corporate control, and even a reversal of corporate personhood, we have bankers and oil executives and

135 Patrick Greenfield, "Revealed: More Than 90% of Rainforest Carbon Offsets by Biggest Certifier Are Worthless, Analysis Shows," *The Guardian*, January 18, 2023, https://www.theguardian.com/environment/2023/jan/18/revealed-forest-carbon-offsets-biggest-provider-worthless-verra-aoe.

136 Patrick Greenfield, "'Nowhere else to go': Forest Communities of Alto Mayo, Peru, at Centre of Offsetting Row," *The Guardian*, January 18, 2023, https://www.theguardian.com/environment/2023/jan/18/forest-communities-alto-mayo-peru-carbon-offsetting-aoe.

137 John Vidal, "The Tribes Paying the Brutal Price of Conservation," *The Guardian*, August 28, 2016, https://www.theguardian.com/global-development/2016/aug/28/exiles-human-cost-of-conservation-indigenous-peoples-eco-tourism.

the International Monetary Fund promoting "carbon offsets" and "net zero" as the solution to atmospheric climate disruption, none of which means zero emissions or stopping pollution.[138] It would seem odd that financiers are promoting "solutions" to the problems caused by their very financing, but carbon marketing is a scheme the Big Greens came up with and have promoted relentlessly, thanks to exorbitant funding. This explains why the latest fad, "nature-based solutions"[139] (code for more carbon offset schemes) is lauded by Shell Oil and the like.[140] More recent fads include the jargon of "climate smart" and "nature positive," all said with forceful assuredness and a tone of comfortably removed optimism. Nice words. Meaningless words. Rather laden with meaning that centers business interests first. In this scenario, greed is called "intelligence," and greedy people are called "saviors" and "experts."

Whales, elephants, and now wolves are being equated with carbon metrics for the carbon market, reduced to numbers just like they have typically been reduced to blubber, ivory, and bounty. Only now in the name of climate change saviorism. "Researchers estimated that the presence of wolves in all boreal forests in the United States

138   "Double Jeopardy Report: How Nature Based Solutions Threaten Food Sovereignty and Agroecology," Friends of the Earth International, November 3, 2022, https://www.foei.org/publication/double-jeopardy-report-nature-based-solutions/.

139   Chris Lang, "Nature-based Madness: A US $1.2 Trillion Carbon Market by 2050?" REDD-Monitor, October 20, 2020, https://redd-monitor.org/2020/10/28/nature-based-madness-a-us1-2-trillion-carbon-market-by-2050/.

140   Chris Lang, "'Worse Than Doing Nothing': Shell's REDD Offsets in Indonesia and Peru," REDD-Monitor, November 18, 2020, https://redd-monitor.org/2020/11/19/worse-than-doing-nothing-shells-redd-offsets-in-indonesia-and-peru/.

would increase carbon storage between 46 million to 99 million metric tons."[141] While these figures might at first glance sound benignly like environmentalists trying to explain the value of ecology to bankers, the problem lies in how the same environmentalists are selling out to bankers. As Cassandra Smithies, author of the exposé "SAVE the Whales...from the Carbon Market," names the problem: "Instead of cutting greenhouse gas emissions at source, polluters want to pretend they can use whales as sponges for their pollution. The United Nations, the International Monetary Fund, 41 countries including the USA, gas and oil industries and 'conservation' NGOs want to perversely turn the last remaining whales into whale offsets for carbon markets – a grotesque greenwash."[142] Nigerian activist Nnimmo Bassey asks the obvious: "The UN wants to use elephants and whales for carbon offsets. Will humans be next?"[143]

Wolves, it turns out, are next.

If wilderness meant home, if wolves were understood as ma'iingan, these economic schemes would have already fallen flat because their conceptual grounding relies on the concept of people and nature as separate, and of life as quantifiable.

Carolina Behe of the Inuit Circumpolar Council of Alaska speaks about how conservationists tend to focus on conserving one piece of the puzzle, while the "greatest points of vulnerability are where

141   Heather Harl, "Wildlife: A Crucial Piece of the Puzzle in the Fight against Climate Change," Defenders of Wildlife, January 17, 2021, https://defenders. org/blog/2021/01/wildlife-crucial-piece-of-puzzle-fight-against-climate-change.

142   "UN Condemned for Whale Offsets: Privatizing Nature for Climate Fraud," Global Justice Ecology Project, November 10, 2021, https://globaljusticeecology. org/whaleoffsets-release/.

143   "UN Condemned for Whale Offsets."

things are interconnected. Pay attention to relationship," she advises, "not just the individual."[144] There is no end to pinning carbon metrics onto trees, wolves, or beavers, for sale. Nor is there definite accuracy. There are ways to account for interrelational restoration, and though the accounting may be more general, it is also far more holistic and true than simple economic quantification.

Dahti Tsetso, representing Dehcho First Nation, asked Dene People to define conservation for themselves. After community talks and thoughtful reflection, the following founding principles of conservation were drafted:

1) Dene law, values, and principles of respect and sharing.
2) Dene language, not English, to explain the Dene perspective of land.
3) Youth and Elder mentorships.

"Being on the land, in the Dene way, will protect the land."[145]

I am interested in knowledge that can't be quantified. That isn't easily bought and sold. Knowledge that doesn't have to be learned the destructive way, wisdom. The specificity in noticing how wolves gathered to watch a plane depart, the long-time cultural recognition of wolves as powerful, integral to healthy caribou herds, to choreographing herd movement. The essential understanding of the mutuality of relationship, of reciprocity. None of which requires a price tag, or an estimate of carbon tonnage, and does not fit neatly

144   "AFC Community-Led Conservation Northern Webinar," YouTube, May 16, 2017, https://www.youtube.com/watch?v=kgmxvnjjwlA.
145   "AFC Community-Led Conservation Northern Webinar."

on a waxy promotional brochure. All of which would be misunderstood, and perverted, through such figures. Because these things are learned differently, thus comprehended accordingly. It is clear to me that perspectives that consider Wolf a relative, hence someone with whom we have a relationship, and for which there are protocols for our part of that relationship, have greater longevity and practical know-how in sustaining life on Earth.

We did not think of the great open plains, the beautiful rolling hills and the winding streams with tangled growth, as "wild." Only to the white man was nature a "wilderness" and only to him was the land "invested" with "wild" animals and "savage" people. To us it was tame. Earth was beautiful and we were surrounded with the blessings of the Great Mystery.

—CHIEF LUTHER STANDING BEAR

IF WILD MEANT HOME

O ur senses evolved in relationship with the (wild) natural world and in contact with other beings. This is noteworthy. The places we live shape our senses and our interpretations of what we see, how we perceive. This means knowledge is at stake when places are destroyed, and when animals who help maintain those places are eradicated too.

In the words of Canadian embodiment philosopher Ellie Epp: "The destruction of beauty, of complexity, of physical coherence, all of these are forms of destruction of mind, that is, of practices of intelligence that depend on the flourishing of the natural world."[146] It was Ellie who told me the full moon of mid-winter is also called the wolf moon. The moon of the longest nights that rises to approximately the height of the midsummer midday sun. Such that if you want to know where the midnight moon will be in six months' time, ask where the midday sun is now. Sirius is also known as the wolf star.

There is nothing as complex, detailed, and minutely stunning as the evolutionarily adapted, coherent complexity of this planet. The intoxicatingly red earth of a dry creek bed imprinted with bobcat and deer tracks. The myriad colors and textures of prairie grasses that

146   Ellie Epp, "Workshop Index, Embodiment Studies Web Worksite," http://www.ellieepp.com/mbo/bodies/workshops/mindlandl.html.

make an autumn walk feel like a trance. The nuanced variations on the color green after rain coats a forest. There is no imitating these evocations of beauty, these conditions for excellence of contact.

American author Leslie Marmon Silko, of the Laguna Pueblo in New Mexico, writes about how place is more important than time. How the specificity of places – whether a mountain peak, a river, or a rock in the shape of a buffalo – holds more significance than the date an event occurred. Territory as in natural geography, the terrain one traverses. And territory with a spiritual dimension, imbued by stories passed on through time, which give meaning and legend to the rocks and the buttes and the river canyons. She tells of how the stories she grew up with instilled a sense of belonging, locating her *within* the story, which was also the same land she roamed horseback as a child. There is no Cartesian duality at work here, as she asserts, no deteriorated view of humans as separate from the natural world.[147]

The idea of "wilderness" as something other than or outside of people that is in need of protecting or, in other words, controlling, comes from a false dichotomy of people as just that – separate from nature. Indigenous People have long since called bluff on this, have called it for what it is, a conceptual framework designed to back land grabs. Nature and culture as separate comes from the same dualism that considers wolves enemies, not relatives. Or otherwise reduces wolves to objects of study, not capable of reciprocal awareness.

Narratives of "untouched" ecosystems and "virgin" territories are imposed by foreigners, fabricated anywhere people can and have lived. Years ago, upon arrival at the Pirá Paraná River, the first thing

---

147   Leslie Marmon Silko, *Yellow Woman and a Beauty of the Spirit* (New York: Simon & Schuster, 2014).

I learned, descending in a bush plane onto a remote dirt landing strip over a veritable ocean of trees, was that relatively every single square mile of the Amazon has been touched by people. Generations of walking, hunting, fishing, as well as cutting and burning down sections of forest for planting gardens before moving on to let the forest grow back, have diversified the canopy one mosaic piece at a time.

Yet here we have the word "virgin" applied to forests people have tended, whether growing manioc in the Amazon, or prescribed burns for acorn harvesting in California. The word virgin echoes the word lupa as a way of saying whore. Next to kicking people off their long cared for homelands in order to "safeguard nature," the concept of "wilderness" or the "pristine" in need of outsider protection has also had the effect of justifying sacrifice zones. Some places matter, others don't. Some people matter, others don't.

European accounts of Australia, before the British and their convicts devastated the continent, were of a verdant and abundant place with plenty of water.[148] Land tended to by skillful caretakers got labeled by foreigners "a wilderness." Relegated as separate from humans, and so altered accordingly. Nuke testing in the outback. Open-pit gold mines.

When I was 17, I moved to Brisbane, Australia, for my last year of high school as a study abroad student. I'd been there once before, at 2 years old, and have had this moment impressed upon me by my parents: myself, a toddler, refusing to leave the red dirt outback while they feigned leaving me there. At high school, we were assigned research projects. I decided to investigate the Stolen

148   Bill Gammage, *The Biggest Estate on Earth: How Aborigines Made Australia* (Sydney, Australia: Allen & Unwin, 2014).

Generation, those vicious years when the state systematically took Aboriginal People's children away. I didn't know much about this parallel history in North America at the time, but somehow I knew just enough to take on this aspect of Australian history and write about the grief and deceit of it, shadow lurking behind Australia's modern self-portrait. I presented in class to a mute room and stone-faced audience. It would take me years thereafter to realize how peculiar and disquieting they must have found this American girl who chose to delve right into the bloody heart of their convict nation, which so resembled my own.

North American environmental historian William Cronon, in his poignant essay "The Trouble with Wilderness; or, Getting Back to the Wrong Nature," writes, "The removal of Indians to create an 'uninhabited wilderness' – uninhabited as never before in the human history of the place – reminds us just how invented, just how constructed, the American wilderness really is."[149] A narrative that was paradoxically coupled with the killing off of wolves, grizzly bears, bison herds, and the long, mournful litany of other creatures whose numbers continue to decline, to disappear entirely. This is the irony: the people who made up the word "wilderness" also decimated so-called wilderness, or were the ones to benefit from this conquest.

European accounts of New York state, before it was "New" "York," noted similar abundance to a once verdant Australia, particularly in the awe-inspiring corn harvests, the fertility of soil. They couldn't believe what they saw. Dr. Jane Mt. Pleasant, Tuscarora national

---

149   William Cronon, "The Trouble with Wilderness; or, Getting Back to the Wrong Nature," https://www.williamcronon.net/writing/Trouble_with_Wilderness_Main.html.

expert on Iroquois agriculture, tells of how Iroquois maize farmers produced three to five times more grain per acre than wheat farmers in Europe.[150] Soldiers who burned their storehouses in military maneuvers were astonished by the yields. A 1687 account witnessed more than a million bushels of Iroquois corn destroyed; it took the army seven days to cut up the corn of only four villages.[151]

The higher productivity is mainly due to absence of the plow, which meant higher levels of soil organic matter. Iroquois maize also has higher yields and was grown in the common Three Sisters companion planting of corn, beans, and squash. Squash vines prevent soil erosion, cornstalks provide beanpoles, and bean plants fertilize the soil. When Euro-American farmers occupied Iroquois homelands at the end of the 18th century, they plowed those lands. They plowed their way westward after each three-year cycle devastated generations of topsoil and resulted in lower and lower yields. The plow led westward expansion – on the heels of buffalo hide hunters and wolvers.

Later, the descendants of these European colonists became the recreationists. Cronon again: "The curious result was that frontier nostalgia became an important vehicle for expressing a peculiarly bourgeois form of antimodernism. The very men who benefited from urban-industrial capitalism were among those who believed

150 Jane Mt. Pleasant, "The Paradox of Plows and Productivity: An Agronomic Comparison of Cereal Grain Production under Iroquois Hoe Culture and European Plow Culture in the Seventeenth and Eighteenth Centuries," *Agricultural History* 85, no. 4 (Fall 2011).

151 Gerald Hausman, *Turtle Island Alphabet: A Lexicon of Native American Symbols and Culture* (New York: St. Martin's Press, 1993).

they must escape its debilitating effects."[152] Ironically, what this has meant since is that the recreationists (again, mostly male European descendants) became the environmentalists and conservationists who have since exported the wilderness construction worldwide through global nongovernmental environmental organizations in league with the corporations seeking to greenwash their "climate footprint." Footprints the size of open-pit gold mines, with cyanide ponds where migrating birds die in search of water. "Only people whose relation to the land was already alienated could hold up wilderness as a model for human life in nature, for the romantic ideology of wilderness leaves precisely nowhere for human beings actually to make their living from the land."[153] This is what conservation as defined by the recreationist, not the local, looks like.

Deborah Bird Rose names how, for the Yarralin People, knowledge and responsibility go hand in hand, which makes for wisdom. Knowledge that is located: "To take care of country is to be responsible for that country. And country has an obligation in return – to nourish and sustain its people."[154] Taking care of land is thus a pact; an agreement between human and place. Wilderness?

The very word "wild," akin to "wolf," has a complex range of associations. Self-reliant, self-willed. No deferring to dominance, no forced dependency. Associated with feral, spirited, uncontrollable. Sometimes used as a synonym for brave, freethinking, fiercely alive. Perhaps in essence it means creative. Though it's also used to mean

152   Cronon, "The Trouble with Wilderness."
153   Cronon.
154   Deborah Bird Rose, *Dingo Makes Us Human: Life and Land in an Aboriginal Australian Culture* (Cambridge, UK: Cambridge University Press, 1992), 109.

trouble, undomesticated, out of control. The word "wild" is often contrasted with control. For whatever diverse associations one may have with the words "wild" or "wilderness," they still fall short in describing care and responsibility.

Wolf is also often synonymous with freedom. Another human construction corresponding to its opposites – entrapment, toil, slavery, servitude, in context with kingdom, hierarchy, possession. Without these dominating forces, would the word "freedom" exist? Would "wolf" be less fraught? I walk circles around the word "freedom" too. The proclamations of free people when structural conditions simply change face. The way freedom is justified through war. The yearning I have always had for that sense of being free, found most often in outskirts places, on a bluff, in the ocean, squinting my eyes into a strong wind.

For the Yarralin People of Australia, to be personally free (in the sense of the English word) is best interpreted as to have one's own will, one's own mind, and to act upon that will.[155] Barry Lopez, after many years, realized that perhaps wild animals should simply be called free animals.[156] In many ways it speaks more to the essence of meaning than wild ever has. Rather than semantic, the problem is conceptual. Insomuch as the word "wild" is close kin to the word "home," it holds water, even though it's hard to let go of the colonial association wilderness has with *terra nullius*, a thieves, lie. Latin

155 Bird Rose.
156 Barry Lopez, foreword to *Earthly Love: Stories of Intimacy and Devotion from Orion*, by Alex Carr Johnson, Kathleen Dean Moore, and Teddy Macker (Great Barrington, MA: Orion Society, 2020).

for "nobody's land."[157] Still, in many ways wild and wilderness (in English) are all we've got for calling on something less regulated and controlled, places where free animals roam.

In the high north, radiation fallout sickens seal, reindeer, and therefore the people for whom these animals are sustenance. Not even that far away from city, smokestack, and highway. Because winds travel, move air, move toxins, across oceans. Arctic waters used for testing nukes, dumping grounds. Nations vying over minerals in Greenland and Antarctica. Corporations betting on ice melt to open up shipping passages, bribing access for more oil, more mining. Land and Ocean and People treated with abandon. These stories surround us, no matter where we live.

Canyon lands. Back roads. Far upriver and over the mountain pass. Be sure to make it before first snowfall. Follow deer tracks and paw prints, claw marks pointing the way.

Think Wolf.

Think like Wolf.

And don't look back.

157 "*Terra nullius,*" Wikipedia, https://en.wikipedia.org/wiki/Terra_nullius#cite_note-Klotz1998-1.

The path to the wild beyond is paved with refusal.

—JACK HALBERSTAM

CHOREOGRAPHY

Ever since the early part of the 20th century, when wolves became virtually extinct in the lower 48 states, they've found their way south from Canada a few at a time, tending toward trailing along the Continental Divide and crossing into Montana and Idaho. Although Marcus told me about a time he saw a white wolf in northwestern North Dakota. Apparition or spirit perhaps, flash of a long-legged canine near Writing Rock, the carved stone that rests on a lookout knoll bearing the ancient petroglyph of a Thunderbird.

Nevertheless, if a few wolves get established anywhere across the west, they are usually isolated from one another. In this way it is hard to make a real comeback. In 1974, gray wolves were added to the US federal endangered species list, affording them much needed protections, but still by the 1980s only a handful of survivors remained in the continental United States. This is why reintroduction was so important. Long a dream for many, in the mid '90s reintroduction became a reality.[158] Politics lined up, and wolves were let loose in the Northern Rockies.

In 1995, the Fish and Wildlife Service introduced 41 gray wolves from Canada back into the continental US. The majority, 34 wolves,

158   Niemeyer, *Wolf Land*.

went to Yellowstone National Park, the first wolves whose howls were heard echoing after some 60 years. This is because a few short years after Yellowstone was originally established, people got to work poisoning off the wolves. By 1926, the last known Yellowstone wolf was dead.[159]

The remaining seven wolves were let loose in the Idaho wilderness, where on a crisp January morning a convoy of trucks drove down the Salmon River road toward its end at Corn Creek in the Frank Church – River of No Return Wilderness to deliver the first reintroduced wolves into Idaho. Crates were hoisted from the truck, the doors lifted, and three wolves bolted out, while one refused to move, snarling and terrified.[160]

In Yellowstone, wolves were let go in three separate locations throughout the park. The logistics were complicated, an entanglement of wolf biology, typical bureaucracy, and heated politics. All the while requiring international agreements with both Canadian and US customs, identifying likely packs and the mechanics of trapping, holding and shipping, as well as the challenge of handling the media and people working cooperatively across many different agencies.[161] Still, it happened. And in 1996 more wolves were released in both locations, with a total of 66 wolves released across the Northern Rockies.[162]

159 Van Tighem, *The Homeward Wolf*.
160 Jim Dutcher and Jamie Dutcher, *The Hidden Life of Wolves* (Washington, DC: National Geographic Society, 2013).
161 Renee Askins, *Shadow Mountain* (New York: Anchor Books, 2013).
162 Dutcher and Dutcher, *The Hidden Life of Wolves*.

Wolves have practically no protection in Canada.[163] The wolves were taken from Alberta in a virtual free-fire zone, where trappers are allowed to trap anywhere on Crown land. A Canadian reference to its legacy tie to England, otherwise meaning "public" land.

Each trapper was paid $2,000 for every live, uninjured wolf. Initially, there were problems with the snaring equipment, which was faulty, but there was also the problem of trappers unaccustomed to trapping wolves to live, not die. All but one, who had his heart in it.

Carter Niemeyer, as much an old-fashioned trapper as anyone after a 20-year-long career with Animal Damage Control, later turned Wildlife Services, had become a trapper to collar and release wolves, and a man dedicated to try to protect the same animal he'd become so skilled at taking out. Having the uncharacteristic quality of compassion toward wolves, while also skilled in coordination among the Canadian trappers, Niemeyer is attributed with ensuring far fewer wolves died in the process of this historic mid '90s wolf reintroduction.[164]

Being that the whole of Alberta is divided into registered traplines, nothing about this was simple. Most local trappers were unaware or disinterested in the reintroduction project to the south, with a few exceptions. Once word came that a trapper had a wolf in a snare, they had to act quickly, as keeping wolves alive wasn't part of the usual trapper's know-how. So when Niemeyer got a call one late afternoon, he drove through the night to retrieve what wolves he could, shoot them with sedative, not bullets, in order to make sure

163   Niemeyer, *Wolf Land.*
164   Askins, *Shadow Mountain.*

they would make it on those planes headed south to Yellowstone National Park and the Idaho wilderness.

A half-Danish, half-Greenlandic woman I met in Nuuk once told me something interesting about sedating polar bears. The polar bear in a zoo, if sedated, will act unlike any other animal waking up. They will not twitch, kick, or awake drowsy but rather wait, silently, until regaining full consciousness and rise with hunter's speed intact. Wolves wake more slowly; they open their yellow eyes.

Niemeyer wrote a memoir called *Wolf Land* that tells of his work helping reintroduce wolves to the lower 48, and his experience of going from trapper to wolf advocate. The memoir is full of accounts of trapping wolves across the west. He describes driving trucks with sedated wolves sleeping on his lap and setting traps with stink brew, while making sure the clamps are padded enough so as not to break a foot. Of finding pissed-off wolves in the brush, he writes about having to load a syringe pole quickly in order to poke the wolf with enough sedative so he could get to work, whether transporting the wolf (and sometimes pups) to new terrain and/or fitting a collar on with the hope of keeping an eye on the wolf's whereabouts and thus (hopefully) helping to keep the wolf alive. He took care in setting traps for the weight of a wolf, to minimize the chance of catching anything else, whether bobcat or bear, and was diligent about checking them daily, at dawn, so a trapped wolf wouldn't have to endure the stress of being captive for too long.

From mid-November to mid-December, in that early winter of 1994, 17 Alberta wolves were snared or darted, fitted with radio collars, and released so that, when the actual collection phase in the new year began, their packs could be located.[165] These were the "Judas" wolves, only in this case not to kill. A month later, biologists would return and with the help of the trappers collect the wolves for reintroduction.

The political maneuvering that happened around the initial reintroduction of wolves was extreme and cunning. The Farm Bureau, for instance, waited until the wolves were in midair to file a request for an emergency stay with the US Court of Appeals in Denver, Colorado. It was an attempt to demand the wolves not be released even into the acclimation pens, and ideally get them sent back to Canada, which wouldn't accept them in any case. This meant once the captured wolves finally arrived they were legally forced to remain in their kennels. A fury of public outcry led to prompt dismissal of this monkey wrench, and the Yellowstone wolves were released into the acclimation pens, while the Idaho wolves were hard released without having to wait in enclosures.[166] By 2005, the population of wolves in the continental United States exceeded 1,000,[167] and yet the wolf epic continues.

On April 14, 2011, the United States Congress made the unprecedented decision to remove an animal from the Endangered Species list. The gray wolf. This would happen again in 2017. It happens under red or blue administrations in the US context, it happens with dismissal. Until the 2011 decision, delisting was a tedious process, requiring scientific review and consensus of multiple government agencies. Unsurprisingly, the wolf became the exception. The

165   Askins.
166   Askins.
167   Scott Kublin, "A Friend of Wolves for Decades," Earth Justice, https://earthjustice.org/features/a-friend-of-wolves-for-decades.

delisting itself never came up for a vote. Instead, the legislation was intentionally buried deep within the federal budget bill as an unrelated rider.[168] By the spring of 2012, Idaho's wolf population had been cut in half.[169]

In January of 2017, senators from Minnesota, Wisconsin, and Wyoming introduced a bill called the "War on Wolves Act" that would further strip federal protections from wolves and allow trophy hunting and trapping in their three states, as well as Michigan. All of Michigan's federally recognized tribes oppose wolf hunting.[170] Wyoming has the most hostile management program, allowing for unlimited shoot-on-site killing across 85 percent of the state, a "predator zone" effectively everywhere outside the Yellowstone park ecosystem.[171]

In February of 2020, the first wolf hunt in seven years took place in Wisconsin, despite an outdated state wolf management plan and inadequate regulation of the "harvest." Within just two days, hunters with packs of hounds overshot the quota by 119 wolves, and the hunt was closed, while reports of wolf kills continued. It was a free-for-all, and the Menominee and Chippewa tribes were never consulted.[172]

The Chippewa oppose wolf hunting because, according to their own cultural hunting practices, they do not manage wolf packs

168   Dutcher and Dutcher, *The Hidden Life of Wolves*.

169   Dutcher and Dutcher.

170   Kelly House, "Lawsuit: Michigan Wolf Advisory Groups Stacked with Hunting Advocates," Great Lakes Now, April 9, 2021, https://www.greatlakesnow.org/2021/04/lawsuit-michigan-wolf-advisory-group-stacked-with-hunting-advocates/.

171   "Congress Unleashes War on Wolves," Earth Justice, January 18, 2017, https://earthjustice.org/news/press/2017/congress-unleashes-war-on-wolves.

172   Helena Wehrs, "Wisconsin's 2020 Wolf Hunt: What Went Wrong?" *The Daily Cardinal*, March 18, 2021, https://www.dailycardinal.com/article/2021/03/wisconsins-2020-wolf-hunt-what-went-wrong.

through hunting. Ma'iingan is their brother. "It is based on our traditional science, from our Elders, that whatever you shoot, you eat," Marvin Defoe, representative of the Red Cliff Band of the Lake Superior Chippewa has explained. "I've never eaten a ma'iingan."[173]

The urgency of this topic, the wolf, is evoked daily. Not just through the slim-margined votes in Colorado for reintroduction of wolves into their state, but in the minds of us as people. Such kill lust is out there, poised and ever waiting for regulations to shift, as they do, in erratic and often compromised ways.

Still, against all fear and cynicism, wolves are returning through human help and of their own accord. And in Yellowstone, in particular, the return of wolves demonstrated a visceral change in the health of the land. Rivers swelled, and beavers are again busy at work in the channels. There are more birds. Elk remembered how to move with frequency and stay alert. Grass in the meadows has thickened, and aspen forests are growing tall. Wolf songs echo.

173   Wehrs.

Loba: symbol of lake water

yellow moon eyes
ricochet

WORDS FOR RESTORING
TO BALANCE

After wolves were poisoned out of Yellowstone National Park, after the Shoshone, Bannock, and other tribes who have called this land home for centuries were made into trespassers,[174] park authorities started killing off the elk in mass. Because, without wolves, their population exploded, and then the grassland, the aspen groves, the willows, began to disappear. Without willows, beavers vanished. Without beavers, streams eroded into silt floodplains. Without the aspen groves, other animals vanished too. Ground nesting birds couldn't find safe haven in grass that never grew tall enough to shelter their nests.[175]

The terms "trophic cascade" and "keystone species" were penned by American ecologist Robert T. Paine, who spent most of his career studying the interactions of food webs in rocky intertidal ecosystems of the Pacific Northwest. The main point: predators help keep the land, and ocean, intact.[176] The metaphor of the keystone is to

---

174 David Truer, "Return the National Parks to the Tribes," *The Atlantic*, May 2021, https://www.theatlantic.com/magazine/archive/2021/05/return-the-national-parks-to-the-tribes/618395/.
175 Van Tighem, *The Homeward Wolf*.
176 Peterson, *Wolf Nation*.

say that, without that essential stone holding the arc of the bridge in place, the bridge will collapse. Trophic cascade conjures up the image of a waterfall and means something akin, the set of reactions that course through a food web, stemming from the presence or disappearance of the top predator, who, in this metaphor, determines the flow of the river.

Removing predators from a region does not safeguard herd animals, because maintaining balance is complex and interrelated. American hydrologist Robert Beschta, studying the effects elk have on rivers, or in other words the hydrologic degradation that was happening in Yellowstone caused by such intense browsing, says it plainly: "Herbivory is perhaps the most underrated force in ecosystems across the world. If people really knew how much plant communities have changed following the loss of major predators, they would be shocked."[177] Grasslands and also aspen groves – those beautiful, white-barked, northern trees with fluttering leaves that spread through their roots. A small stand of aspens is likely a single plant. Each trunk a stem of one organism connected underground through an expansively entangled root system. If no younger stems are able to reach maturity, delicacies as they are to grass-eaters, then the older stems eventually die, and the grove disappears.[178]

It's simple: herd animals aren't complacent when wolves are around, or able to outnumber the land's capacity. Like otters in the ocean. I can now stand along the familiar rocky inlet to Morro Bay, on the harbor side of the break I surfed growing up, and watch sea

177   Cristina Eisenberg, *The Wolf's Tooth: Keystone Predators, Trophic Cascades, and Biodiversity* (Washington, DC: Island Press, 2013), 172.

178   Moskowitz, *Wolves in the Land of Salmon.*

otters roll around making slick circles in the water, crack clams on their bellies, and tangle themselves up in seaweed so they can sleep and not float away with the tide. I do not take their company for granted. Sea otters once ranged from northern Japan to the Aleutian Islands, all the way down to Baja, California. Yet, by the early 1900s, they were nearly extinct due to large-scale commercial hunting for pelts, including Russian military hats, with as few as 13 colonies remaining, and on the California coast a mere count of 25 found in Big Sur. The 1911 North Pacific Fur Seal Treaty came into effect, and slowly the population began to increase.[179] Today, there are perhaps 3,000 otters living in the inlets and bays across California's rugged coastline.

Otters hunt in nearshore kelp beds, and without them everything changes. Sea urchins, a staple food source for otters, will eat away at the kelp beds until nothing is left but an "urchin barrens," [180] the marine equivalent of overgrazed hills, where instead of a tapestry of grass, there is dust. Where there is no kelp, there is no fish, hence no food for birds, whether seagulls or eagles, depending on how far north along the Pacific coast you are. Reach the islands off the coast of so-called British Columbia, near the Great Bear Rainforest, and you'll encounter a subspecies of gray wolf that has adapted to a maritime life of eating mostly seafood, salmon heads, hunting seals, and chewing on barnacles. Known as Gonakadet by the Tlingit, and

179   Eisenberg, *The Wolf's Tooth*.
180   Eisenberg, 59.

Wasgo by the Haida, these ocean wolves can swim for miles between islands, among the otters and what few orcas remain.[181]

Where wolves disappear, coyotes increase. Coyotes who are adaptable, skilled at living in the narrows between forest and city street. The coyote I saw midmorning, walking up the sidewalk in San Francisco. The three traipsing at dusk through the city's Presidio state park. Coyotes have filled in most of the wolf's former range across the North American continent. Medium-sized predators, classified *mesopredators*, take over where "keystone species" are killed off. When coyotes increase, it puts abnormal pressure on smaller animals, like birds, which can even become extinct.[182] Coyotes hunt small rodents, so with too many coyotes, raptors like eagles and ospreys have less chance at a meal. Loss plays out in countless ways, and every loss makes the world more diminished.

When wolves returned to Yellowstone, the expression of a trophic cascade was vivid. People celebrated the simplicity of it: wolves returned, and the land flourished. Of course, nothing is so singular. To a mind that craves so-called silver bullet or blueprint solutions, this is frustrating. To scientists vying for the power to name, to take credit, this is a perfect chance to argue over theories and one-up one another. It is also ridiculous, utterly ridiculous, that the obvious has to constantly be appropriated and renamed.

While professor and biologist Michael Soulé may state the following with great conviction – "trophic cascades science provides

181   Peter Faris, "Wasgo/Gonakadet – Sea Wolves of the Pacific Northwest Coast," *Rock Art Blog*, September 25, 2018, https://rockartblog.blogspot.com/2018/09/wasgogonakadet-sea-wolves-of-pacific.html.
182   Eisenberg, *The Wolf's Tooth*.

copious evidence for concluding that the unpredictable, devastating, downstream effects of apex predator removal, particularly herbivore and mesopredator release, are major drivers of global ecological collapse"[183] – the trophic cascade theory has still been challenged. Wolves are understood as one among several influences to reducing elk populations and changing their grazing patterns. Growing bear numbers and drought are others.[184] Yet fighting over the particulars of Soulé's statement, the validity of the keystone concept, whether top-down or bottom-up forces prevail, or the details of how trophic cascades happen, only stalls the process of returning, protecting, calling home.

183   Eisenberg, 213.
184   Peterson, *Wolf Nation*.

Where the River Longs to Touch the Ocean

:::::::::::::::::::::::::::::::

Land language perforates
at the confluence of three rivers

cholla cactus, curtained sorrow
candlelight and a choir that sings clean water

tomorrow is another word for warning
frack another word for torch-the-dawn

there are people who will extinguish
anything that smells like freedom

plow up the grasslands
watch the world unhinge

the wolf, the child riding bareback
fast as a northerly, the sound of a drum beat

sunset red as Bing cherry
a wash of purple lupines

deer hide tipi and an old Cadillac
asphalt cracked

beads of rain string phosphorescence
across the paintbrush limbs of a Japanese maple

intention can turn particles to waves
ripple light across galaxies

ARCTIC HYSTERIC

To be critical of the dominant, and therefore interrogate it with the dominant language (perhaps, in particular, in written text), is to imply being positioned within or imbedded one way or another inside this force. The force that has broken continents, exterminated, upended, appropriated, and misunderstood. The force that has romanticized and criminalized Wolf. Hence, criticism must involve the self.

In the timeless essay, "Ethno-Aesthetics," Greenlandic-Danish artist Pia Arke reminds me of this. Also how increasingly rare it is to not fall into either/or, to be strictly "us" v. "them." Arke embodied and demanded autonomy in this third space, a mixed place, undefined (though she called it "mongrel," with humor in her eyes). It was the 1990s when she wrote down her thoughts. Post-colonialism was center to the discussion – Europeans increasingly reckoning with the theme. "Post" itself a fallacy. Perhaps in part why she chose the title of her essay to begin with, and because it is a "messy concept that inspires further work."

Pia Arke:

So, Western appropriation and marginalization of the alien is constantly at work. You may want to stress that postcolonialism is an intellectual invention combining postmodernism and anti-colonialism in a way that conceals the continuation of colonialism by other forms of suppression and exploitation of the Third World. However, this is not an insight that in itself will transcend the regime of Western intellectualism from which it has sprung.[185]

Of her homeland, Kallalit Nunaat, she writes: "It is the projection of Western order with its claim to categorical and essential purity up against the cultural flea market of modern day Greenland."[186] And, with stunning accuracy: "At this point, I would like to interject that, more than anything else, this whole matter is about Europe. Ethno-aesthetics is an opportunity for dealing with the real thing: European culture with its aesthetics, its ethnography and its reason. It is a way of 'involving oneself,' a mixed-up way, but first and foremost a possible way."[187] Europe: Where wolf became werewolf. Where wolf became devil. Where these ideas traveled from, touring the world entire.

I could quote Arke's whole essay, but you'll have to find a copy for yourself. I am lucky because Marcus has a sharp eye for books, and in a bookshop in Nuuk he noticed the thin-bound copy in a muted red, simply with black font. Coincidentally printed by ARK press. In the intro, the Danish editors acknowledge as much gleefully. It is just thick enough to look like a poetry book because the essay is translated into English, Kalaallisut, and Dansk. It is a kind of poetry.

185   Pia Arke, *Ethno-Aesthetics/Etnoæstetik* (Copenhagen, Denmark: ARK, 1995), 27.
186   Arke, 23.
187   Arke, 13.

I later learned that, in the spring of 1995, Arke went to New York City. There she dug through the archives of the NYC Explorers Club, where she came across a photo from Robert E. Peary's collection of an Inuit woman, half-naked and screaming, "being restrained by two fur-clad and seemingly untroubled white men."[188] A curator told Arke that the woman may have been suffering from "Arctic hysteria." But when Arke asked for the rights to reproduce this 85-years-out-of-date photo, the club declined her via fax, calling the image "too sensitive to reproduce."[189]

Peary, famed Arctic "explorer," is known for his desperate lust for fame and the self-proclaimed title of first person to reach the North Pole. Whether or not this is true, he got close, thanks to the practical know-how of Inuit People, who he was (unlike many early European explorers) smart enough to learn from. He wore furs, slept in an igloo, and traveled by dogsled. Yet, despite his total dependence on Inuit knowledge, as well as skilled labor, he described Inuit People in typical derogatory fashion: "keen-eyed, black-maned inhabitants of an icy desert; simple and honest, occasionally sulky; wandering, homeless people: these are my children, the Eskimos."[190]

Peary is also responsible for the particular form of hysteria Arke was introduced to when she found that photo of her kin. He took an Inuit word, which he spelled "piblokto," a word meaning a range of things from "madness" to "drum dance fit" to "to be starving," depending on the context, but which Peary attributed to hysteria.

188   Vanessa Gregory, "The Unforgettable Pia Arke," *Hakai Magazine*, February 14, 2017, https://www.hakaimagazine.com/features/unforgettable-pia-arke/.
189   Gregory.
190   Gregory.

Running with the sexism self-proclaimed as intelligence of the time (and still, pitifully, is today), Peary reduced a range of experiences, where he may well have been witness to ritual or rebellion, physical illness or depression, to one singular psychiatric label. Enter: Arctic hysteria.

Psychoanalyst A.A. Brill, who headed Columbia University's clinic in psychiatry and first translated Sigmund Freud's writings into English, substantiated fiction through sexist prestige. His 1913 theory designated the cause of Arctic hysteria as "a childish fit thrown by a woman who does not get her way."[191] He also emphasized the placement of "Arctic" next to "hysteria" as specifically Inuit. Hence, an even more derogatory, demeaned form of womb sickness. The word "hysteria" originates from the Greek word for uterus and somewhat ironically has been associated with the supposed weakness of the feminine mind, even though the uterus is the strongest organ with a veritable mind of its own during childbirth. Brill claimed, "Civilized women suffered more complex hysterical attacks," whereas Inuit women threw "primitive tantrums." In his words: "There is hardly anything more childish than the imitation of the dog or bird, or the running away into the hills singing and crying."[192]

This haughtiness lives on, as do the lies. It is convenient, of course, a narcissist's trick, to dismiss all context in order to place sole blame on the person, often the woman, who is fighting for her life. And in classic colonialist master fashion, pit allied people against one another with trite distinctions as to their belittled differences. On Peary's expeditions, and in his camps, Inuit women

191   Gregory.
192   Gregory.

labored as slaves, expected to "sew, fish, carry wood, and submit to the Americans' sexual desires."[193] There are accounts that describe women as intent on escape or dissent, lunging for the ship's railings, shouting for a knife. The obvious fact is that these women were not crazy. They were brave. They were rational. They were reacting like any brave, rational woman would.

One might have said the same about the women once called werewolves.

Arke, in artistic response, created a video called *Arctic Hysteria*, a performance lasting six minutes in silence and consisting almost entirely of one scene: Arke crawling naked across a giant, black-and-white photo of Nuugaarsuk Point, Greenland. Where she lived as a child, outside the small town of Narsaq. In the film, Arke strokes the photo, rolls across it, and smells it. Then she rips it to shreds, gathers the debris of paper, and lets it fall like snow over her shoulders and thighs.[194]

Home embodied, home in shreds. Language of action and silence.

In Kalaallisut, there is no word for resilience. As in climate resilience. As in jargon for how to endure global colonial economic empire's wreckage. As in abstraction. As in comfortably removed theorizing over the end of the world, as we know it. I mean, really, what is meant by climate resilience?

Survival.

Inuit People know how to survive. On ice. How to greet the sun for one moment, peeking through midnight darkness, and slowly,

193   Gregory.
194   "Pia Arke. 'Arktisk hysteri,' 1996," YouTube, https://www.youtube.com/
      watch?v=K2OeiTTuty8.z

daily progressing toward the luminous, all-out, midsummer sun. All northerners know some version of this, the further north the more defined. That and aurora. The Greenlanders I met, when asked about the shifting climate and the fast-melting ice, were less concerned with climate change than rules and regulations imposed by the outside. Of "resilience," they said, well, huh. The closest word is something like how to live/living life.

And isn't that it, *how will we live?* On the land, across the water, through drought and thin sea ice. Because all the fancy tech fixes and market schemes are only making more of a mockery of what's already the greatest, human-caused, yet bigger than all of us, disruption on Earth.

How will we live?

With common sense, perhaps. Some wit and kindness and style. Without forgetting our origins, our ancestors. The ways we are complicit and wounded. With aesthetics, I'd like to think, harkening back to Arke. With aesthetics. Because it is honesty that we need, which means specificity, to the best of our respective capabilities, in whatever languages we speak. Honesty that requires understanding, learning what those forces of dominion sought/seek to erase. The word for wolf, translated to mean guide, relative, friend. The word for echo, echo, echo. Remember. Do not forget.

Pay attention to what they tell you to forget.

—MURIEL RUKEYSER, "DOUBLE ODE"

THE WOLF PACK

Wolf culture is centered around kinship, pups, and the pack. Wolves will mother orphaned pups as their own. Like all mammal babies, wolves dream in the womb to create visual circuits in the eyes for when they open their eyelids. Born blind and deaf, pups' eyes open at ten days to two weeks of age. They are weaned some five to nine weeks later, when they begin to eat regurgitated meat brought back to the den by adult wolves in the pack. Wolf rendezvous sites have been described like living rooms, resting areas where wolves gather and reunite, where puppies play. The kinds of pup toys brought home by adult wolves include moose antlers, highway cones, leather boots, bear skulls, and random bottles or cans. All with tiny punctures made by puppy teeth.[195]

Gordon Haber mapped out the underground structure of the Toklat pack's home site in Denali, Alaska, by crawling into each of the dozen or so tunnels that made up the den area. He found wolf dens clean and dry, lined with a thick layer of wolf underfur, soft bedding for pups. Home sites, Haber learned, were one of a cluster of dens within an eight-mile radius. He figured the wolves moved from one to another to help train their young to travel. Comprised

195   Niemeyer, *Wolf Land*.

not just of dens but lookouts, interconnecting trails, and play areas. Tunnel entrances usually faced south.[196]

In Cochiti Pueblo, Wolf is considered a timekeeper, the spirit that leads the people through the seasons. The very structure of community mirrors a wolf pack. A-dae Romero-Briones explained this to me once. In her home community, leadership is understood in community terms, concerned with the well-being of the whole, much like wolves. In Cochiti, she explained, people are born either for the summer or the winter, represented by the Kivas. The Turquoise side is connected to the winter and winter solstice. The Pumpkin side is connected to the summer and summer solstice. Together, the village is complete. Wolf, as Timekeeper, journeys, and in these travels keeps time and balance between the two seasons, while maintaining the pack through the change of seasons. Wolves also model leadership by placing the strongest, most able members at the back of the pack, who then become responsible for the more vulnerable members in the middle. The elders are in the front, setting the pace and tone. The pups are in the middle, protected by all. In this way, the health of the community is maintained through social organization and consistency through the change of seasons.

Leadership in the top-down formation, as that of asserting one's dominance, and not centering the youth and children, not locating people where their knowledge and skill can support others, is quite prevalent these days. Assertions of dominance don't work well with

---

196 "Among Wolves: Gordon Haber's Insights into Alaska's Most Misunderstood Animal," Wolf Conservation Center, October 17, 2013, https://nywolf.org/2013/10/among-wolves-gordon-habers-insights-into-alaskas-most-misunderstood-animal/.

"wild" animals, only domesticated. Because asserting dominance is not a way to relate.

Domestic: Of or relating to the home, to household affairs. Existing or occurring inside a particular country, boundaries defined, a passport required.[197] *Tame*: Not dangerous, not "frightened by humans." Docile. Submissive. According to a *Merriam-Webster* dictionary search: "Reduced from a state of native wildness especially so as to be tractable and useful to humans."[198] Notice the word "reduced."

Oddly, many people call this kind of nonreciprocal behavior – of asserting authority – a form of exerting control, "leadership." Assertions of dominance, of domination, of supremacy – the world right now is sick with this. A boring and unimaginative, tyrannical yet peculiarly adolescent, way of being. A manner that does not work well if you want to relate, grow trust, be stronger together, or otherwise consider the health and well-being of future generations. The problem with a supremacist mind is not just a matter of justice; it is a grave limitation in imagining other ways of living.

In Rick McIntyre's words, the true alpha male wolf demonstrates "a quiet confidence and self-assurance...You know what's best for your pack. You lead by example...You have a calming effect."[199] Certainly, not *alpha* in the way Wall Street traders refer to stock sheets. Investments as *deals*, which would make the whole industry of profiteering this way a kind of game. *Game*. Poker, horseshoes, billiards. *Game*. Animals hunted. Caribou *crops*. Wolf hunt *quotas*. Language and how we use it. Language and how we misuse it.

197   "Domestic," Dictionary.com, http://www.dictionary.com/browse/domestic.
198   "Tame," *Merriam-Webster*, https://www.merriam-webster.com/dictionary/tame.
199   Peterson, *Wolf Nation*, 66.

I remember the first time I accompanied foresters to a monoculture Oregon forest and listened to them discuss board foot, lumber. I was working for an environmental NGO and had joined the forestry crew to get a sense of their department. These men saw themselves as sane, competent managers of forest, and while they weren't clear-cutting, I had a hard time seeing them as much different from the lumber companies deforesting entire hillsides, causing landslides, raking in profit. While their practices were more conscious, their language was the same. It was a language that ignored life, the quality of ancient presence and nonverbal intelligence one feels in an old-growth forest, and which even science is catching up with in comprehending. The ways trees talk to one another, for instance, which people have long since accounted for. In this case, the forest had become a factory.

This is why the translation of Wolf as guide has meant so much to me, imbued as it is with a different metaphor. That of guiding the pack toward health and safety.

A *Senunetuk*: a whalebonewolf hunter
creates a whalebone arrow
in a Z pattern, he gently slides the sharp end
into walrus blubber, freezes the fat
whole, then places it in a trapline.
A black-tipped silver wolf eats the frosted *muktuk*.
Thawing in the stomach, the dart springs,
piercing the membrane lining.

      Isibru: a whalebone wolf slayer
      oblique holes for eyes in a wooden
      mask with a dancing gorget rises to the hunt.

—DG NANOUK OKPIK,
"WHALEBONE WOLF HUNTERS DANCE," *CORPSE WHALE*

WOLF-LIKE WISDOM

The wolf taught people how to live, which means the wolf taught people how to hunt. Buffalo, for instance, how to run them off the cliffs. At Head-Smashed-In Buffalo Jump in the Alberta high plains of Canada, here's how it went: a young man (being initiated as a hunter) wears an auburn buffalo calf hide and imitates a wounded buffalo calf, while two older hunters wearing wolf furs press in on the herd from the back. The herd, concerned for the young calf, goes to surround the wounded calf. The wolf hunters, edging closer, cause anxiety, and as the herd nears, calf-boy leading them toward the cliff, the tribe comes out from hiding to initiate a stampede. Calf-boy running, leading the thundering hooves, has to dash out of the way just before the herd, in rapid-fire stampede, goes careening off the cliff.

This was how people on the plains hunted before the horse arrived. How they survived the long winters, and blizzards, where winds can be harsh as oceanic gales, kicking up swirling dust storms of snow. Bison meat then, as now, fed people. What scraps were left went to ravens, vultures, and wolves. Bones made tools, utensils, and weapons. The warm fur became clothing, the hides tanned and used to make tipis. The fat turned into soaps, hair grease, and pipe sealer.[200]

My friend Sonja Holy Eagle, artist and shopkeeper, paints buffalo hide drums and whole tanned bison hides in traditional mandalas and designs. Her store smells of sweetgrass, sage, and buffalo fur. She once showed me a dried buffalo testicle made into a rattle. Shook it, with a grin. Sonja was the one to tell me when a wolf had just been sighted traversing the Black Hills. Years later, when I told her about this book on wolves, she shared some Lakota wolf stories, as well as names involving wolf from her language, and then mentioned a wolf book, a special copy she'd let me borrow. As she reached for a bin packed beneath the display case, I watched her pull out a well-read copy of Barry Lopez's *Of Wolves and Men* from amid a stash of porcupine-quill Medicine Wheels. I stood there, stunned by the synchronicity, telling her how this was the very book I was reading when the idea for this story took hold, only perhaps having more to do with wolves and women. "Well, I suppose we have this in common too," she responded, smiling.

In hunting cultures, wolf traits are admired: courage, tracking skills, endurance, intuition. The Toklat pack alpha wolves who had the deft skill of hunting Dall sheep and knew in detail the contours of Denali rimrock. From *Of Wolves and Men*, by Barry Lopez:

200 Justin Franz, "A Native Homecoming: The Blackfeet Lead an International Effort to Return the Bison to Their Natural Landscape on the Rocky Mountain Front," Flathead Beacon, April 13, 2016, http://flatheadbeacon.com/2016/04/13/a-native-homecoming/.

An old Nunamiut man was asked who, at the end of his life, knew more about the mountains and foothills of the Brooks Range near Anaktuvuk, an old man or an old wolf? Where and when to hunt, how to survive a blizzard or year when the caribou didn't come? After a pause the man said, "The same. They know the same."[201]

Human and wolf, esteemed equals. I am interested in a world in which that holds true. I also respect this form of knowledge. Observation skills that result from keen attention to nuance, detail – the small things. Knowledge earned from a devotion to the present moment. Eyes trained to notice. A life of training senses, attentive to weather, season and cycle, can make for a kind of psychic quality, a knowing of things that may seem unknowable. An ability to sense accurately. Discern, foretell. Wisdom that can, and has often been, mistaken for magic.

The San People of the Kalahari are known for this knowledge. Renowned as the best trackers in the world, they follow more than prints in the sand, guided by impeccable awareness, comprehensive ecological expertise, and fine-tuned instinct. Knowledge that has been revered, and also demeaned, to preference a mindset with more tendencies to exploit. Today, game preserve fences dissect and corral San homelands. Diamond mines plunder.

Inuit People also rely on hunting; this is how one survives in the Arctic. Yet, since the mid-1980s, they have borne the burden of save-the-fluffy-cute-seal campaigns. They live off seal meat and

201   Lopez, *Of Wolves and Men*, 86.

wear sealskins, polar bear, and sometimes wolf too. Inuit People have high fashion; their attire is downright beautiful. They also sell sealskins from the seal they eat to make money. Seals are harvested by deft hunters who know how to traverse the frozen Arctic terrain, and tanned by mothers and grandmothers in their kitchens and backyards. The meat is still their main staple.

Alethea Arnaquq-Baril produced the film *Angry Inuk*, where she turns soft-spoken rage into story, calling out how these save-the-fluffy-cute-seal campaigns have made Inuit small commercial outfits exceedingly difficult by successfully swaying sealskin bans across Europe. Their bluff stories have profited multimillion-dollar environmental nongovernmental organizations at the expense of a dignified lifeway. Spotted seals, unlike wolves, white rhinos, or blue whales, are *not* on the endangered species list. And, conveniently enough, when the Inuit hunter providing for his community is blamed, the oil titans who want to drill along the coastlines are given headway. The interests of a few individuals for whom the dominant economy serves.

In 1904, in *Harper's Monthly*, Ohiyesa (Charles A. Eastman, M.D.) wrote the essay titled, "First Impressions of Civilization." He reflects, "In civilization, as it appeared to me at first – 'Will it pay? Can I make anything on it' seemed to be the 'Great Mystery' of the white people."[202] In this same essay Ohiyesa writes about being often asked, "Was it not wonderful to you when you first saw the lofty edifices of great cities, the locomotive, the steam-engine and the like?" To which he responds, "in a way," and reflects on the towers

---

202   Ohiyesa, "First Impressions of Civilization," *Harper's Monthly Magazine*, March 1904, p. 587.

of the Bad Lands, and the artistry and constructive genius of the animals – spider, muskrat, ant, beaver, and swallow – who dam and bridge streams and build their homes suspended in air.[203]

Ohiyesa, like Pia Arke and many others, critiqued the dominant culture that he also lived thoroughly, while embodying the memory, wisdom, and perspectives of his upbringing immersed in culture that did not/does not conform to this hegemony. It seems that the essence of this critique is simply to demand the Other exist equally. Other, in both cases, actually *original*. Local. Indigenous: sprung from the land. Hence, the word "dominant" to begin with. The colonial empire is a colonial empire because its language and education and religion and political and legal systems became that, dominant. Dominated the worlds of others. Dominated the world. Not because its trappings of culture were better but because they were forced. As forced as the dogma surrounding Wolf that I sit here peeling apart like a bulb of garlic.

Al Thieme, an elk hunter himself, reflected: "Only when we as a culture can experience the ability to hold two contradictory concepts in our minds simultaneously about wolves will we be able to allow them to thrive fully, and not limit the number of wolves in the ecosystem to serve the interests of a few individuals."[204] Individuals for whom the dominant economy serves.

This is to say that wolf-like knowledge moves counter to the interests of a few, moves with fluidity and deftness, with instinct and relationality, with grace.

203 Ohiyesa.
204 Moskowitz, *Wolves in the Land of Salmon*, 229.

∧∧∧

Skull 1 shattered. ground into powder and used for ammo. death made visible in pilings. wolf skulls tossed in with bison skulls on rail cars headed east from westward deterioration. things unaccounted for. 2 I have deliberately offered a bison skull to the prairie. smeared in red earth. showered with white sage. 3 when Comet died, the black and white speckled longhorn steer given to me by a neighbor rancher on my christening day, I tracked down his skull. followed vulture flight, circles in the sky. he'd left the herd, walked up the long dirt road, lain down in a steep bank gulley thick with poison oak. his skull now hangs, a relic, an honoring, a cavity for birds to nest. 4 the particular size of a cranium. people reduced to data, measured as other-than the predetermined norm. 5 a baby's skull is not fully formed, that's how we fit through the portal.

THE BIG LIFE

I rode in a seatless van across the Mongolian steppe once, in the company of herders passing around a bag of fresh mountain blueberries and a sheep that was shitting on the metal floor. All our teeth were purple, and we couldn't help but smile. The sheep's scat rolled around like marbles.

The month I spent wandering around Mongolia impressed upon me deeply: The taste of fermented horse milk. The strength it took to ride horseback in a wooden saddle, and the way children raced bareback, fast as wind. The prayer flags tucked away in forests where people go to gather pine nuts. The Khazak man I met in a *ger* selling mutton soup to travelers, who offered me bear lard ointment for the callouses on my heels from cheap leather boots and long days of dusty walking, explaining as much through theatrical hand gestures and sounds. So, when I learned that one of the best-selling contemporary Chinese novels was a book about Mongolia, I was curious.

Titled *Wolf Totem*, and written by retired professor Lu Jiamin, initially under the pen name Jiang Rong (Jiamin participated in the Tiananmen Square protests and was thrown in jail for a period of time), the success was unexpected in China. Its popularity so great, the book soared past censors who consider it severely anti-Communist.

Jiamin's jail stint wasn't reason enough; the main reason for censorship is because the book celebrates Mongolian culture. A herding/ hunting culture, contrary to the predominately agrarian nation of China. It also commends the illiterate or semiliterate military leaders of the Mongols – as well as the Jurchhens, Huns, Tungus, and Turks – who all at different times, but most notably under the leadership of Genghis Khan, brought the great Chinese military to its knees. Attributing their skills and fortitude to none other than the wolf.[205]

Skills of guerilla warfare aside, what comes through most strongly are awe and respect for a people and a lifeway that has been marginalized and oppressed by an industrial agrarian empire. The vigorous, bureaucratic forces of the Cultural Revolution, adamant about killing off the wolves and plowing up the fragile Mongolian grasslands to farm, have resulted in yellow dust. Yellow, billowing, dust clouds. Because when there is no protocol, it is easy for people to take more than they need. For the Han immigrants to the grassland, it took one season to turn a nesting lake for swans and other birds into a lifeless water trough. To hunt down an entire generation worth of marmots. The story echoes the memory of North America's Great Plains, Australia's outback, places where colonists arrived without restraint, respect, or knowledge of a place locals had long since called home.

Wolf Totem is set in the Olonbulag, southwest of the Great Xing'an mountain range and north of Beijing, sharing a border with Outer Mongolia, a place that was historically the southern passage between

205   Jiang Rong, *Wolf Totem* (New York: Penguin Books, 2008).

Manchuria and the Mongolian steppes. The main character, Chen Zhen, alongside a handful of other Han Chinese students, is sent to Inner Mongolia in 1967, the height of China's Cultural Revolution, to work. A Mongolian old-timer, Bilgee, teaches Chen how to live as a nomad, which also means teaching him about wolves. In China to this day, wolf tongues are sold as medicine to soothe a sore throat, while some people believe that storing four wolf legs and a wolf skull in your home will bring good luck in card games.[206]

Old man Bilgee is at the heart of the novel. His yurt is described as a space "the Red Guards' fervent desire to destroy the Four Olds – old ideas, culture, customs and habits – had not yet claimed."[207] The yurt's walls are adorned with Mongol-Tibetan religious tapestries, the floor covered with a rug of a white deer design. Bilgee's is a wise voice. He speaks for the grasslands and the wolf: "Out here, the grass and the grassland are *the* life, the big life. All else is little life that depends on the big life for survival." Grassland, the big life, is also the most fragile. "If you rupture its grassy surface, you blind it, and dust storms are more lethal than the white-hair blizzards. If the grassland dies, so will the cows and sheep and horses, as well as the wolves and the people, all the little lives. Then not even the Great Wall, not even Beijing will be protected."[208]

Bilgee is himself one of the most adept wolf hunters, with restraint. He does so out of need, when wolves attack his sheep herds or horses. "Protecting the grassland is hard on us. If we don't kill

---

206 "The Himalayan Wolves Project," WILDCRU, https://www.wildcru.org/research/the-himalayan-wolves-project/.
207 Rong, *Wolf Totem*, 22.
208 Rong, 234.

wolves, there'll be fewer of us. But if we kill too many of them, there'll be even fewer."[209] He is referring to the ground squirrels, rabbits, marmots, gazelles, sheep, cattle, horses, and field mice – the little life who eat the grassland and can destroy the grassland if unchecked. He speaks of trophic cascades and keystone species, without using this jargon.

In evolutionary terms, the Himalayan wolf is considered an ancient lineage of wolf and has been largely overlooked by scientists.[210] It has uniquely adapted to the low-oxygen environment of the 4000-meter elevation of the Tibetan Plateau, Himalayas, and Central Asian highlands.

Similar to the Tibetan sky burial, where the deceased are offered to high plateaus for the vultures to feast on, Mongolian tradition has held sacred the tradition of offering the dead to the open steppe, to the wolves. Wolf pelts are worn for warmth but never for bedding, which would be an offense to the Mongol gods. Wolves are considered the protective spirits of the grasslands, spiritually but also literally. The Dukah People of Northern Mongolia, a reindeer people, rely on wolves to keep life in balance. They see wolves as teachers and protectors, teaching them to be good herders and protecting both their reindeer and the other animals of the taiga by preventing the spread of disease.[211]

209 Rong, 123.
210 "Protecting the Mysterious Himalayan Wolf," Future for Nature, December 9, 2019, https://futurefornature.org/protecting-the-mysterious-himalayan-wolf/.
211 Jennifer Sherry, "In the Taiga, Livestock Herders and Wolves Strike a Balance," Natural Resources Defense Council, October 4, 2019, https://www.nrdc.org/experts/jennifer-sherry/taiga-livestock-herders-and-wolves-strike-balance.

Mongolian reverence and elemental respect for wolves as herders is noteworthy, when the typical hatred is tied to wolves killing livestock. This is not to say Mongolian herders don't kill wolves, they just don't kill *all* of them, for their knowledge of wolves holds a deeper wisdom than that. By tradition, when a wolf first takes an animal, "it's seen as a blessing, an offering to the ecosystem that supports the herders." Only if the wolf pack takes additional animals will the herder hunt the wolf.

American wildlife biologist Rebecca Watters, who has worked in Mongolia studying wolves for over 20 years, reflects upon her own experience in how "American wolf luminaries will tell you, disregarding your fluency in Mongolian, that you must have misunderstood, that Mongolians, as a herding people, *must* hate wolves." She hits on the duality in the center of all this and asks: "How many of us are capable of living across this spectrum of understanding?"[212]

A main thread of *Wolf Totem* is Chen's determination to raise a wolf pup, and how his love for the pup, and fascination with the untamable nature of wolves, is what also causes him to torture the wolf by never letting him go. Unheard of on the steppe, it infuriates Bilgee, who has great respect and admiration for the wolf and cannot accept the thought of treating a wolf like a dog. Trying to describe to Bilgee why he wants to raise a wolf, Chen says, "I want to figure out why they're so formidable, smart, and why the people revere them. You can't imagine how much the Chinese hate wolves. We call the most malicious people wolves; we call sex fiends wolves;

212   Rebecca Watters, "An Ancient Rural Culture Deals with Wolves Halfway around the World," Mountain Journal, February 13, 2019, https://mountain-journal.org/mongolians-have-an-ancient-relationship-with-wolves.

we say the greediest people have the appetite of a wolf; the American imperialists are referred to as ambitious wolves; and anytime an adult wants to frighten a child, he cries out 'Wolf!'"[213] And isn't all that just right there at the center of the typical reputation of wolves?

The predatory wolf-man, "wolf of Wall Street," is a classic association and also one I feel less in need of examining. It is offensive and also ironically celebrated. Hitler himself co-opted the image of Wolf like he stole the swastika and Thor's hammer. His first secret Eastern Front military headquarters, with personal bunker, was called the Wolf's Lair, sited in the Masurian woods in present-day Poland. His own self-adopted nickname was Wolf. A Russian motorcycle club with deep ties to the Kremlin, flamboyantly anti-gay, and that even contributed to the invasion of Crimea by patrolling the peninsula, call themselves the Night Wolves.[214] I find it cheap, frankly. I consider these aggressively masculine overtoned wolf rip-offs vile and absurd and also not as underhanded as the way certain people are deemed wolf-like, in need of subjugating.

In 2020, the Chinese government began a campaign to take down Tibetan prayer flags from the Tibetan Plateau.[215] Pedestal of the world. I traveled there at 17 with a group of students a few years before visiting Mongolia. This was before the "friendship train," well after the Chinese invasion. According to the visa in my passport, I was in China after all. Our bus driver snuck firewater from a flask regularly. In the monasteries on occasion, monks would

213 Rong, *Wolf Totem*, 271–272.
214 "Night Wolves," Wikipedia, https://en.m.wikipedia.org/wiki/Night-Wolves.
215 "Tibetan Prayer Flags Forced Down by Chinese Authorities," International Campaign for Tibet, June 18, 2020, https://savetibet.org/tibetan-prayer-flags-forced-down-by-chinese-authorities/.

whisper in secrecy that Dalai Lama's photo was hidden behind the fake Panchen Lama. I played a game of soccer with Tibetan kids while wearing my hiking boots, the air thin, sun bright. I noticed the bullet holes in the paintings of deities in abandoned buildings.

This moment: Midday in the high plateau city of Lhasa, in conversation with a Tibetan woman, a dialogue of gesture and eyes. She gives me a pewter ring from off her finger, the shape of a heart framed simply in the center of the band. I give her a tiny abalone shell strung on a leather cord from around my neck.

On March 10, 1959, Tibetans rose up against Chinese occupation. Every year since, Tibetans the world over reaffirm their call for freedom. I joined one such gathering in front of San Francisco City Hall with my infant son in his baby backpack on my chest. The speeches Tibetans gave were solemn and grave, with too-oft-used words like "torture."

At the Minneapolis hockey stadium, I once heard His Holiness the Dalai Lama give a lecture. He repeated two words with particular emphasis: *secular ethics*. I don't know how secular ethics translates into Tibetan, but what I do know is that his voice sounds like a very powerful melodic drum when speaking in his mother tongue.

These end times we are living – end, another language by the fortnight, species by the day – became acute in my own foresight out there on the plateau. And it was this, perhaps more than anything: Tibet without Tibetans peaceably in their homeland means the peak of the world is being ransacked, forests cut down, rivers dammed. Rivers running from the highest place on planet Earth to nourish the vast plains and valleys and fields of Asia. Nothing could be a more symbolic stranglehold of the empire mind. Then, after and amid everything, a campaign to rip down the prayer flags that traverse river canyons and adorn high mountain passes, carrying prayers and mantras through the wind – there can be no end to lengths people will go to disappear one another, along with the rivers and the big life and the wolves.

Hot butter tea and *tsampa*. Wild blueberries and *ayrag*. A cold wind blowing. Prayer flags tattered and fluttering, fluttering. Glimpses of life in old rhythm. Glimpses of how the world would unravel. And yet, and yet. The stories of wolves and the wisdom of peoples who have been exiled like wolves are sought out by the many of us who want to remember.

Loba: sense of imminence

circular split-shadowed
　　　　　　　　vanishment

KILL FOR FUN,
OR LIVE ALONGSIDE

Echo was the name given to the recent apparition who arrived in northern Arizona. Except, she wasn't an apparition at all but a wandering gray wolf. She traveled at least 450 miles from her original home, wearing an inactive radio collar that suggested she'd traveled from Idaho, Wyoming, or Montana to the North Rim of the Grand Canyon, where wolves were eradicated by the 1930s. These were the same years the Havasupi were forced from their home, relocated to an Indian work camp to work for the railway, their summer village burned to the ground by the Park Service.[216] Echo crossed highways, roads, and private property. Then, in 2014, she was shot by a hunter in Beaver, Utah. *See wolf, kill wolf.* She acquired the name through public consent, public inspiration, and endearment. First wolf in 70 years. Many people want wolves to return, there is a longing that's palpable, a hunger. I think simply because we are relatives.

216   Opheila Watahomigie-Corliss, "Uranium Mining Threatens Our Home, the Grand Canyon," High Country News, April 14, 2020, https://www. hcn.org/articles/indigenous-affairs-mining-uranium-mining-threat-ens-our-home-the-grand-canyon.

And there are people for whom the wolf remains a target, because they were taught the ugly wolf fear and hatred narratives. Even those who may well know wolves are not this reduced, this simple, are still trying to deconstruct.

"Back there you shoot, shovel and shut up." This is the classic thing people say. Of the man I heard it from, a campground host on a plateau overlooking Rapid City, South Dakota, he added the following about wolves he'd seen with his own eyes: "Them wolves vanished. Two near Mobridge [a town just south of Standing Rock, along the Missouri River]. Big as deer." It is often that short, that simple. Wolves disappeared in places that are also disappearing, whether to urban sprawl, a fracking boom, or the plow.

On this same plateau overlooking Rapid City I meet the eyes of a mountain lion for the first time in my life. The sound of someone crashing into barbed wire. A twang and rattle. I cock my head sideways, casually, departing a frontward gaze into tangerine flames. I sit on a bench next to Marcus, the lone campers in a campground with a row of self-contained RVs. Out of the shadows: a cougar, round face glowing by campfire light. In the time it takes to hold a breath, I stare, thoughtless, for a long dreamlike moment, before registering who had emerged from the night and is standing five feet in front of me. The cougar stares back unflinchingly at both of us. Until, on impulse, we stand, hit by a delayed recognition of the hunter in our midst. A presence so commanding. And in that same instant the cougar flees. Flash of tawny fur bounding away into shadows. The neighbor turns up the volume on his television. The fire crackles. Cars continue to barrel by, white headlights heading southbound, red lights glowing and then receding to the north. By the flame of a tea light in a mason jar, I collect hair from a single barbed wire, the lowest strand, to remind myself this had been real. I place two soft blonde strands into a tiny plastic bag with crumbs of sage for safekeeping.

I was raised in a valley of live oak woodlands, coastal sage, and chapparal. Cougar habitat. Ample places to hide, track, hunt, find refuge. I was always told to take the dogs with me when I went hiking. That and to make myself big in the case of an encounter, which as a child seemed ridiculous. Stretch your arms out wide and yell like a drunken sailor. I never saw one. Not once. And then here, in a campground run by a host who'd just been telling me about dead wolves, there I was, eye to eye with a mountain lion, with a face like the sun.

Mountain lions are far more dangerous, and yet far more common these days, than wolves. Which again makes me wonder about wolf hatred. The ruckus of it, the hype. I'm not of the mind for killing a mountain lion, or wolf, because they ate one calf. I am also talking about something deeper, something irrational, inherited, and largely unexamined about the subconscious reasons people say *see wolf, kill wolf*.

Often called on to deal with pissed-off and frightened people mistaking a dog's paw print in snow for that of a wolf, Carter Niemeyer has used his authority as a trapper on many occasions to talk sense. On multiple occasions, Niemeyer has had to point out tire tracks and the reality of cattle rustling as reason for lost cows, otherwise death from dehydration or eating poisonous plants, which happens to cattle, only it doesn't have the same flare as a wolf kill, or is not as exciting and convenient a source of blame. He sums it up this way: "Maybe livestock interests are too powerful. Or maybe most people are just unaware that the system still operates as though the West is still being settled."[217]

It is an irony to me that ranchers, people who often live closer to a land-based ethic than many these days, are disproportionately pitted against the wolf in their politics. Steadfast people holding fast to the tether of relative freedom their cowboy life affords, adamant about that ideal of freedom, and somehow anti-wolf. These are people who live for a lifeway, who could sell their land and make millions but often don't, who persist through drought, through many rugged uncertainties. Yet still will often recklessly shoot coyotes, bobcats, cougars, wolves. Given the pervasive forcefulness of these attitudes, states continue to delist wolves from the Endangered Species Act when ranchers' losses are small due to predators compared to drought, wranglers, sickness, poisonous plants, or perhaps more than anything, developments that cause their taxes to rise. When the costs of helicopters and aerial sharpshooting, strychnine and traps, exceed sensibility or basic economic logic, it seems they might just want someone to blame.

Bison blamed for spreading brucellosis (there is no known account of bison transmitting brucellosis to cattle).[218] Wolves blamed for [fill in the blank]. The state of Washington has had some notable success bridging between wolf advocacy groups and ranchers, effectively working out strategies to protect cattle herds and wolves. What this really means is face-to-face, well-moderated dialogue, people seeing each other as people, not as enemies espousing opposing

217   Peterson, *Wolf Nation*, 12.
218   Ruth Rudner, *A Chorus of Buffalo* (Short Hills, NJ: Burford Books, 2000).

ideologies. An overarching issue here is land ownership and who that entails. Euro-American people. My family included. Factually, and disturbingly, Euro-Americans own 98 percent of rural land in the United States.[219] Until this changes, all the talk will circle around convincing certain people to think differently. Ridiculous arguments will ensue, and some common sense understandings will take place. Still, it is a frustrating waste of time having to convince people who don't really want things to change.

Examples of active management include guard dogs; flashing lights; red, flapping strips of cloth hung on fences; range riders. Herd instincts to stand ground and group together against predators help also, which heritage breeds tend to still have more intact – akin to muskox or buffalo.

Complacency isn't worth the extra marbled meat in the big scheme of things. But this is one of the many ways industry interests have directed living conditions too often against life. The grassland needs grass eaters. What we don't need is a meat industry that confines cows to their own manure, or overgrazes hillsides to dust. What we don't need are wolf hunts where so-called hunters kill 216 wolves in a matter of days.

This kill happened in Wisconsin in 2021. The ease of killing came through state permission to use hound dogs. The quota state regulators had set was 119 wolves. After two and a half days, hunters had almost approached the limit, and before the kill could be shut down,

219   Antonio Moore, "Who Owns All America's Land? A USDA Report Is Exposing a Massive Disparity between White and Black Land Ownership in the United States," Inequality.org, February 15, 2016, https://inequality.org/research/owns-land/.

another couple days later, 216 wolves had been shot. When hounding wasn't allowed, it took trappers and rifle hunters over two months to kill a similar quota target. This time it took just over a day. Hound dogs in this case meant six at a time, with fresh dogs substituted as the others tired, making it impossible for wolves to outrun their pursuers. That and at least a dozen men in camouflage, likely with one wolf permit between them, vying for the singular shot. A vivid image of how pathetic a gang pitted against one can look. [220]

Rod Coronado is the founder of Wolf Patrol. Yaqui and an animal rights activist, he is a nemesis for these Wisconsin houndsmen. He trails the hunters in the backcountry with his radio and camera. He documents this so people will know and share in his revolt. [221]

No human has been attacked by wolves in the state's modern history, and the Wisconsin deer herd has been above management goals for years. Similar to Yellowstone and western Wyoming, after the wolves returned, the wolf population in Wisconsin has remained steady, in sync with the elk or deer herds. Wolf populations are inherently self-regulating, if anything sending wanderers elsewhere to establish new packs. Yet Wisconsin alone has a law requiring an annual wolf hunt, like Wisconsin alone allows hound dogs. Flyers advertise coyote and wolf hunts as casual as Budweiser ads, and often with a tall auburn glass of beer printed in the corner, double advertising. "That was fun" is why these people kill wolves. "Real fun." [222]

220 Nate Blakeslee, "'An Abomination': The Story of the Massacre that killed 216 wolves," *The Guardian*, July 27, 2021, https://www.theguardian.com/world/2021/jul/27/wolves-winsconsin-massacre-environment-conservation.

221 Blakeslee.

222 Blakeslee.

Thus, wolf "management" is in response to people's beliefs about wolves, their fears, their statistics, their tall tales and debauchery, otherwise their kinship.

Leslie Marmon Silko has an entire chapter in her memoir *The Turquoise Ledge* devoted to rattlesnakes. She lives on the outskirts of Tucson, Arizona, buttressing national forest right out her old ranch house door. She lives among the rattlers and has learned to love them. Of close calls with rattlesnakes coiled up beside her adobe flowerpots, she does not blame the snake. Rather, she accounts for her own lack of paying acute enough attention to her surroundings, placing value on this high quality of perceptiveness, and equally the intelligence and particular role of the poisonous snake, without whom she would have that many more gophers and pack rats sneaking into her kitchen for food. Of the old-timers she knew as a child growing up in Laguna Pueblo, she writes how they would sprinkle corn pollen or ground blue corn into the circles snakes made in the sand, as well as the paw prints of mountain lions. And how the old stories tell of giant, 12-foot-long rattlesnakes, respected guardians of sweet water springs after whom pueblo potters coil-build to mimic the rattler's spiral coil.[223]

Kill for fun, or live alongside. The stories we hold define how we act. The metaphor of Wolf, in this way, is a precise mirror reflection as clear as lake water harboring the moon, depending on the metaphor one chooses.

223   Leslie Marmon Silko, *The Turquoise Ledge: A Memoir* (New York: Penguin, 2011).

Poetry is a mode of thinking. What if we opened ourselves
to more and different modes of thinking?
We'd probably be less murderous.

—TONYA FOSTER

THE ABILITY TO TRANSFORM

At the Canadian Museum of History in Quebec, there is a small ivory carving of an upright female form with a wolf head fashioned by the hands of a Tuniit craftsman, ancestor of the Inuit from the central Arctic.[224] Feet apart. Arms dropped at the hips. Slender waist. Wide hips. Pointed jaw. Big ears.

Clarissa Pinkola Estés, Mestiza Latina author of the classic *Women Who Run with the Wolves*, tells the story of La Loba, the old Wolf Woman. She who is ancient and knowing, a wanderer practiced at remaining unnoticed. With a home hidden in the outskirts, or simply an unsuspecting place that few people will ever encounter. La Loba is a bone collector, gathering "especially that which is in danger of being lost to the world."[225] She wanders up arroyos and into the mountains in search of bones. Wolf bones in particular. And what she finds, she carries home to her hearth, to assemble fireside, carefully placing one bone with another. After she has restored a skeleton whole and intact, she sings. This is how the wolf returns to being, and this is when the wolf runs. And always somehow in the motion of the wolf racing free, whether by sheer speed regained or

224 Savage, *Wolves*.
225 Clarissa Pinkola Estés, *Women Who Run with the Wolves* (New York: Ballantine Books, 1992). 23.

simply the quality of light on fur, the wolf transforms into a woman, laughing, as she runs toward the horizon.[226]

Transformation is at the heart of many a story about wolves. Whether people becoming wolves or wolves becoming people, or whales, or perhaps most ancient in memory, simply the friendship, kinship, of people and the wolf.

Orcas, or killer whales, the largest member of the dolphin family, are also known as "sea wolves." Sea wolf, the meaning isn't arbitrary. Their behavior is very similar. Both the orca and wolf are hunters, devoted to their families, and also have close affinity with humans. Orcas have also been similarly projected upon, associated with supposed wolf-like malevolence, made out to be ferocious and liable to attack human beings at any opportunity. Speaking of orcas in 1910, William T. Hornaday, director of the Bronx Zoo, said the following: "This creature has the appetite of a hog, the cruelty of a wolf, the courage of a bulldog, and the most terrible jaws afloat."[227] These kinds of ridiculous misappropriations by Euro-America persisted until the "capture era," when a generation of orcas was taken from their families to be put on display in aquariums.

It started in 1965, when Namu, the orca named after the fishing town in British Columbia where he was stolen from, was towed in a floating pen to the Seattle Marine Aquarium, his family trailing right alongside for over 200 miles, and even slamming against the cage to try and help him escape.[228] Namu showed people how Pacific orcas are, and he died within a year of being captive. Another

226   Pinkola Estés, 23–24.
227   Calvez, *The Breath of a Whale*, 100.
228   Calvez.

example of learning the destructive way. It took devastating an entire generation of orcas to teach newcomers to this continent that, like wolves, orcas are more akin to people than the contrived rogue "killer" they were made out to be. With wolves, of course, this lesson is yet to really land.

Maquinna (Lewis George), hereditary Chief of the Ahousaht First Nation, recounts his people's understanding of the wolf/whale: "Wolves are really a sacred being for us. In our belief the wolf transforms into a killer whale. We feel that the wolf and the killer whale are one in the same creature."[229] When asked what's so special about wolves? And, moreover, why do humans have a different relationship with them than other carnivores? His response was, "None of the other animals that I know of have the ability to transform. That ability is very special and unique, and it's healing."[230]

Within the Yupik tradition, it is known that the beluga whales once lived on land, so in exchange for offering oneself to a Yupik community, the beluga expects its bones will be given ritualistic treatment to allow its return to land, as a wolf. Whale fetuses briefly develop legs before losing them again.[231]

In the Japanese animation *Wolf Children*, a boy and a girl are born of a woman and fathered by a man who shape shifts into a wolf. Their dad is killed (for being a wolf), and their mother moves to the countryside to raise them alone. In growing up, the children begin to feel torn between their two distinct lineages: human and wolf. In

229   Moskowitz, *Wolves in the Land of Salmon*, 235.
230   Moskowitz, 238.
231   Krista Langlois, "When Whales and Humans Talk," *Hakai* Magazine, April 3, 2018, https://hakaimagazine.com/features/when-whales-and-humans-talk/.

the story, the girl eventually chooses to be human. The boy goes to the mountains, becomes a wolf.[232]

There is another transformation in *Wolfwalkers*, an Irish animation directed by Tomm Moore and Ross Stewart, the third and final installment of Moore's Irish Folklore Trilogy, following *The Secret of Kells* and *Song of the Sea*. All stories that depict love and instinct, spirituality and belonging to the animate world. *Wolfwalkers* is about a father and daughter, the father hired from neighboring England to serve authoritarian Irish Lord Protector as his wolf killer. The daughter, trailing her father into the woods to escape the confines of a village centered on religious hierarchy and the felling of old-growth forest, encounters wolf girl.

The two are rivals, but soon become friends, and when the English child wakes up in her loft a day later, she realizes she has become a wolf child also. The wolf girl had healed her with wolf magic, giving her the ability to transform. With the skill of the wolf, she could be free, run like the wind, and follow scent farther than sight, yet now she was an outlaw. Her father, the hired man, doesn't recognize her. She must learn to use her transformation carefully.

Wolf girl's mother, also a wolf-human hybrid, is trapped by the lord during her transformation as a wolf. She is a possession he uses to intimidate the village folk, fully aware of her power. She is his conquest he wants to force into submission and in this way assume power that is not his own. The two daughters work together to free her. Afterwards, the wolf killer for hire joins his daughter and her friends, becoming a wolf himself.[233]

232 *Wolf Children*, Wikipedia, https://en.wikipedia.org/wiki/Wolf_Children.
233 *Wolfwalkers*, Wikipedia, https://en.wikipedia.org/wiki/Wolfwalkers.

In *Princess Mononoke*, the famous Japanese animation by Hayo Miyazaki, two of the main characters are a forest princess and a giant white wolf. Like many of Miyazaki's films, the story centers around animate gods in response to the forces of reckless human consumption – whether industry or war, fiercely intertwined. The term *mononoke*, or もののけ, is a Japanese word for shape-shifting beings that can possess people and cause suffering, disease, or death.[234] San, the wolf rider, has renounced human society. Her nemesis is Eboshi, who is devoted to the people of Irontown, named as it is for the ore the community unearths at the expense of natural law. The Forest Spirit, a deer-like creature with antlers as prominent as the fan of peacock plumage, offers healing and renewal even through death.

My friend Lorraine Nez shared this true story with me about a relative of hers: In the late 1800s, a Sicangu Lakota tipi camp was attacked by militant settlers and burned to the ground. Only a baby survived. When the murderers were gone, wolves arrived. They found the infant and took her with them. A few years later, another Lakota family group was traveling through the area and encountered a cave – the wolves' den – where this child was found crawling around. The wolves allowed her people to reclaim her. Once grown, she was known to camp at the edge of the village where the wolves could visit her, but also because her strong sense of smell was overwhelmed by village life. She had received the skills of scent and sight from the wolves, and so became a healer who knew when and where her help and medicine were needed. She could smell sickness

234   *Princess Mononoke*, Wikipedia, https://en.wikipedia.org/wiki/Princess_Mononoke.

and, with this knowledge, bring medicine for healing. She also had the eyes of a wolf, capable of seeing at night. There were times she would travel by night to skirt enemy territory, accompanied by the wolves who protected her and helped keep her fed. To this day, she is remembered as the woman who lived with wolves.

Blood Road

·

//\\

Trace a path
cut by razor blade
toward the smell
of fresh caught herring
sight of oncoming squall
drone of bombers
sour scent of bloodshed
poker face & swollen tears
pain is an entwining
the burial grounds
where gravestones mark
oval ship hulls
()()()
the burial mounds
plowed over
to plant wheat fields
all this survival
all these wounds
& vats of coarse
sea salt
chew
plantain leaves
spit
salve
into these
many woundings
\\//

·

DARING TO QUESTION

Ancestors on my father's side were on those early ships that set sail for so-called America, part of that early wave of immigration. My mother is a Danish immigrant. I am the daughter and granddaughter of the ones who stayed and the ones who left. This means my people on both sides come from Northern Europe. This means I've had to ask myself, why did our people leave?

The reasons: war, famine, starvation, religious subjugation, trauma, conquest, greed, fallout of empire. Not the most glorious of reasons. Not the most "civilized."

Of Australian colonists landing on those shores and proceeding to colonize, Deborah Bird Rose explains their denial of murder and land thievery as "a distortion of their own assertions to an identity as well as of their relationships to others."[235] She points out how denial works against the people acting out of it, cutting off the potential for meaningful relationships, other ways of living, being, seeing.

Denial is and has been implicit in the force of colonizing, through the empires of old, the corporations of today. A form of stonewalling, an unwillingness to listen, the blindness by which people couldn't, wouldn't, see the behavioral condition of wolves in North America,

235   Bird Rose, *Dingo Makes Us Human*, 2.

because they refused to. Reminiscent of how Winona LaDuke describes Enbridge company men as nonnegotiable; they won't take no for an answer. No, you cannot trench your tar sands pipeline under our manoomin lakes. How no means yes to rapists also.[236]

I once heard Winona say to a room full of philanthropic foundations, whose endowments hold the stories of colonization, ongoing: "We understand wealth and we understand the appropriation and theft of wealth. Wealth means 500 horses in 1805 traded from the Hidatsa to the Ojibwe and Cree. Thousands of pounds of maple syrup."[237] Stocks that bank on extraction are easier to hoard by comparison, and lack the sweet taste of trees, the warm smell of horsehair.

Colonization: loss of land, language, lifeway, wealth, and the redefinition of wealth toward abstraction, opacity.

Colonization: successfully convincing people not to believe in themselves and in their cultural fabric, their understanding of what holds the world intact.

Colonization: a ripping.

Colonization: Telling people how to "fix things" that were never broken. A shift in decision making, in *who* decides.

Colonization: Silencing, which has a direct correlation with stealing. All the bones and "artifacts" stored in museums. All the ghosts haunting boarding school halls, the pastureland by the creaky old swing set, unmarked graves. Plexiglas and a placard in a cold room made of granite.

236 Winona LaDuke, *How to Be a Water Protector* (Halifax, NS: Fernwood Press, 2020).
237 Winona LaDuke, personal communication with author, Santa Fe, NM, September 2018.

Confiscation and appropriation ongoing.

An addiction to control.

DAPL, Bayer, Halliburton, Enbridge.

Dakota Access Pipeline (DAPL) corporation hired the mercenary firm TigerSwan to carry out military-style counterterrorism efforts in cahoots with local cops.[238] That was how much they feared the drum circles and cedar smoke, the ceremonial fire that was kept burning for months on end at Standing Rock. This is also common practice; corporations have grown accustomed to having cops on their payroll, politicians and oligarchs in their pockets.

I have known moments where it feels like I'm holding a sword, and the people I'm standing off with are sitting in expensive tanks. The sense that these people want to put my soul fire out.

As pervasive as radiation or traces of microplastic. Five hundred years and going. A thing so massive it appeared in people's dreams before those white sails were visible from the shore. That which is a character of mind, a grave capacity for denial, an unwillingness to listen or bend to another's lived perspective and worldview. That which declares Wolf evil. Period.

In angst against the colonial mind, I fight against dichotomy. I come from the culture, the dominant that I critique. I'm there, standing in the room with the crystal glasses clinking and the gloved waiters pouring drinks at long tables with long, white tablecloths, all the wine you can drink and those pretty little sweet and

238   Alleen Brown, Will Parrish, and Alice Speri, "Leaked Documents Reveal Counterterrorism Tactics Used at Standing Rock to 'Defeat Pipeline Insurgencies,'" The Intercept, May 27, 2017, https://theintercept.com/2017/05/27/leaked-documents-reveal-security-firms-counterterrorism-tactics-at-standing-rock-to-defeat-pipeline-insurgencies/.

savory treats. I lean against the back wall, in the far corner of this grand and echoing room, with a stern face and a furrowed brow, arms crossed tightly. I am unable to laugh at the jokes, at the flippant ways life is referred to, quantified. My eyes dart for EXIT doors, skylights, a fire escape. I am phenomenally and disproportionately privileged by this proximity, this position, in this room, stuffy and dank of smell. I have also suffered enough to not take lightly the suffering of people outside. I've taken the blame myself for daring to question.

And in so doing I've been made into Wolf, someone to blame.

The men, who instead of answering a question I raise directly look to another man and say: Why does she say that? What does she mean? Or scoff a haughty laugh in order to avoid responding. What they are really saying is how dare she question me, or my motives. The time my own relative called to mention as much, how the man in this case had approached my family member at a conservation gala, drunk and determined, saying that I'm a problem, that I just don't see the good they are doing. I remember this moment so well, this phone call, because I was on a hill slope in the springtime, rolling up old and rusty barbed wire from where it had slowly, over many years, been absorbed by prairie. With the heavy weight of a roll of taut barbed wire in my leather-gloved palms, I said, "Well, why not just tell him he can talk to me himself."

What anyone who has been garlanded with the metaphorical problem-wolf hide knows is that the ones doing the scapegoating need this image of Wolf, this *lupa*, this mythic creature so thoroughly projected upon as to be an idea, made up, to conveniently shoulder their own unrequited feelings for them. And that this is a pattern that has consumed the world, so the kings and queens, the princes and princesses, can feast and lounge and blame the were-wolves – whose labor and land they stole. I say this as one who is also incapable of fitting nicely into the confines this mind has created.

In the Blank Page I See a Snowdrift

1.

Out of the blue, it seemed. Like a sundog on a clear day.
Tipis and cedar and sage smoke the texture of fog. Inter-
tribal prayer gathering in the center of North America.
Out of the blue. A memory. Death on a cold winter day.
Out of the blue. Oceanic blue. Tall ships. People desperate
and seeking. Out of the blue. Rail ties, steam engines,
stone ballast. Out of the blue. Eastward expansion.
Medicine line, straight as cut paper divides North
America in half. Biggest modern art project, one could
say. Followed up now with another lame version of lime
green steel. Not east to west. North to south. Tar sands
sludge mixed with North Dakota crude, funneled fast and
furious to the Gulf. Out of the blue. Bison slaughtered
with wolves. Treaties denied. Outskirts places. Outskirts
lives. Out of the blue. Oil rigs and gas flares light up
the Northern plains. Satellite images report a new city,
the black center of the continent cluttered with orange
lights aglow. Truckers with plates from every state in the
nation. Man camps. Invasion so huge one could only
endure. Until they tried to channelize. Out of the blue.
Thought they could slip by unnoticed, bulldoze, disregard
a sovereign nation. Thought they'd just get [h]er done.
No. People watched. People have never stopped watching.

People prayed. People have never stopped praying. People called on their relations. We cannot let this demon pass through our territory and contaminate the water! People came. Of course they came.

2.

On a two-lane highway we head northbound.

Grain fields, thatch and sage. Pass decommissioned nuclear missile silos. You can tell by the razor wire. Nowadays storage for hay bales. Keeps the deer out. Rapid City, SD, to Cannonball, ND. At the state divide air masses shift. Humidity rising from the south greets an Arctic cold front descending. A pale blue sky and heavy cloud quilt meet, just as we cross South Dakota into North. Dakota annexed, quartered, by Minnesota wars. Dakota, a people. Dakota means friend.

3.

WATER IS LIFE painted sideways in black ink across someone's front door.

4.

A blizzard is all about the wind. Sideways wind.
Soothsayer wind. Arctic-air-sweeps-across-a-continent
wind. You lean into it to steady yourself. Ice like
snowflakes has structure. Geometric pattern language.
Frozen lakes melt into lattice shapes. Slowly away from
the shore's edge until one morning the ice island sinks.
Under the coat of snow, landscapes return to their natural
contour. Patchwork grids shaped by plow and fence hide
beneath a canvas the color of egret feathers. Ridges and
river bottoms show through in curvature and texture.
Rivers that take the path of a sidewinding snake.

5.

The rosy-faced oilman thinks he can buy his way out of
this one. Like the last one, and the one before. Buy his
fucking way to heaven and beyond. The sky darkens to
the south, pale blue boils indigo, quicksilver clouds. Storm
winds suck into fierce weather. Then switch just before
hail arrives. Hail the size of softballs. Hail that shatters
glass. They told him, you don't want to mess with the
Elders on this one. They meant it too.

6.

Out/of/the/blue. Unexpected. Out[side], out[skirts],
out[sider], out[law], out[yonder]. Of (in reference to). The
(specifically). Blue, color, feeling, water, ocean, water, lake,
water, sky/rain, water, womb water, which we're formed
in. Enter this world [out] [of] a womb taut with salty saline
water. Out-of-the-blue. Creative chaos. Sudden, as if by
magic.

7.

What scares empire most?

We-are-all-in-this-together.

Hot coffee, a warm fire, drum beats, and song.

||||/\||||/\||||/\||||/\||||/\||||/\||||/\||||/\||||/\||||/\||||/\||||/\||||

THE STORY OF WOLF
IS BOUND TO THE
STORY OF BISON

To write about wolves is to write about those who were never meant to survive but have against the odds. This is also to say I cannot write about wolves without writing about bison.

Living in the Black Hills, South Dakota, is where I learned to know bison. In the unceded territory of the Očhéthi Šakówiŋ, the Lakota, Dakota, and Nakota people. He Sapa, in Lakota, means black ridge. Shaped like a heart, they are the roots of ancient mountains, a veritable island in the plains, and have a geographically sacred cosmology for some 50 Great Plains tribes. Specific places across the hills relate to formations in the stars. The highest point, Black Elk Peak, is also the highest point east of the Rockies until you cross the Atlantic Ocean. Thunderstorms hit from every direction, swooping in across the surrounding ocean of land. Entering into daily contact with Tatanka here was a kind of initiation.

I'd drive the red dirt back roads through Wind Cave National Park, put Emmylou Harris on to play. Song number one: "Where Will I Be." Her voice smoky, her songs meant to be played loud. On those slow drives through the park roadways, I'd keep an eye out for herds or a lone bison bull, watch the prairie dogs conduct their sun salutations, and catch the occasional glimpse of a nighthawk's descent as if out of nowhere, slicing the air like a knife.

Bison are earth drummers who can also be as silent as a fox, emerging from behind saplings as if out of nowhere. They are taciturn giants who both walk feather-quiet and stampede powwow drum songs. They face blizzards head-on. Yes, they turn to face the storm.

One afternoon out hiking, I came across a lone prairie rose at the edge of a ponderosa grove. Crouching down to take a photo, I looked up by instinct alone and met the eyes of a bull bison watching me through a sapling a few feet away. I jumped backwards, paradoxically afraid of catching him off guard, when I was the jackrabbit, plainly. We observed each other through the saplings for a long time thereafter. He nonchalant as ever, finding a comfortable place in the dirt to lounge while I leaned against a tree trunk, laughing at myself and grateful for the company.

These are some of the moments that stay with me: a red dirt wallow wet from the last thunderstorm, and a bison bull standing in the muddied dirt, his face painted red from the crimson earth. A mid-winter drive and stopping the car to let some bison cross, the road salted, my car salted, and a huge, scruffy bison head reaching toward the window to lick salt crystals from the hood. That straightforward knowing that a bull bison is near – you can feel it.

Another time, passing through Yellowstone, I spotted a coyote standing in a circle of four bison, as if holding council. Tan and sandy-colored, like sun-thatched grass. Coyote skirted through their circle light-footed and carried on her way.

Plains buffalo: *Bison bison bison.*

Otapanihowin in Cree. "Livelihood" or "means of survival."[239]

The mid to late 1800s mandate was to clear the prairie and make way for progress. This meant that the Great Plains, from western Canada south to Texas, became a slaughterhouse. Agricultural settlement founded in bloodshed. Upwards of 60 million strong until the late 1800s slaughter, bison bones were ground for munitions, their hides made into factory belts, flesh left to rot in the hot summer sun next to wolf carcasses. In the Great Plains, the story of the wolf is closely bound to the story of the bison. Killing wolves went hand in hand with the bison slaughter. Strychnine was the lazy man's tactic, poison the dead buffalo and you poison the wolves. Estimates of 200 to maybe 1,000 bison remained on the continent after this rash extermination. A famine created, a famine ongoing.

Of the plowed-up Dakota prairie turned wheat fields following this murderous time, Marcus, who invited me to live in the Black Hills when he worked as a wildfire scientist at Wind Cave, put it to me this way: "It's like a broken mirror, somehow still beautiful, reflecting the sun, but impossible to put back together again." Another day while driving Highway 385 into Rapid City, he uttered this single offhand line that says it all: "It took this entire continent to appease the desperation of a broken culture."[240]

---

239 Candace Savage, *Geography of Blood* (Vancouver, BC: Greystone Books, 2012), 84.

240 Marcus Lund, personal communication with author, August 2014.

The National Park Service came out of, and eventually in response to, this broken culture, even while it was created by and within it. While arguably crucial to preventing indiscriminate industrialization, and at Wind Cave and Yellowstone serving as refuge for what bison remained, and later wolves, the mythos of pristine and untouched that justified the exile of Indigenous People cannot be forgotten. And this isn't just about resolving the past, because exclusionist thinking whereby people must be "separated from their homelands in order to protect nature" continues to be perpetuated internationally through what people now call fortress conservation.[241]

Killing off the bison herds meant that Indigenous Nations starved. For the Blackfeet Tribe, the winter of 1883–1884 is remembered as a time when more than 500 Blackfeet People, about a quarter of the tribe, died during what has been called "Starvation Winter."[242] The slaughter of wolves and bison alike a method of land thievery. In the words of US Army Colonel Richard Dodge, 1873: "Every dead buffalo is an Indian gone."[243] That was the mandate, the adopted rationale by many an east coast general sent out west. For the whiskey traders, wolvers, and hide hunters, death was banal: another day, another dollar. Gold miners also turned to wolfing, which was easier than buffalo hunting, because all a wolfer had to do was set out strychnine (often in the carcasses of dead buffalo) and gather in the dead wolves at two dollars a hide.[244] Poisoned meat

241 "The Dangerous Legacy of Fortress Conservation," Oakland Institute, April 18, 2019, https://www.oaklandinstitute.org/dangerous-legacy-fortress-conservation.
242 Franz, "A Native Homecoming."
243 Savage, Geography of Blood, 111.
244 Lopez, Of Wolves and Men.

was left out on 150-mile-long ranges during this belligerent period of the late 1800s. The wolvers' motto: "The only good wolf is a dead one." General George Sheridan: "The only good Indians I ever saw were dead."[245]

At a motel in the Cypress Hills in Saskatchewan, Canada, just across the border from North Dakota, I learned that wolvers killed Métis people here. Wolvers. In conversation with a woman at the checkout counter, this sordid fact came up. The things people know and share sometimes as if to share a burden. The things you learn when you take the long roundabout way from the west coast to the center of the continent. They weren't the only ones murdered, of course. The Dakota people also call this land home.

By the early 1900s, hide hunters had to learn how to trap. The lazy fell from wolvers' ranks. Wolf pelts rotted; used only as proof of the kill. Like bison hides had rotted also, their skulls later collected for ammo in war. One does not easily come across a bison skull from the old days left out in the plains. Because while at first the money had come from wolf hides, later it was for bounty. One merely needed to show some body part to confirm the wolf they'd killed. Iowa initiated a bounty law as early as 1838. Colorado, Wyoming, the Dakotas, and Montana followed suit. Montana's first wolf bounty law was passed in 1884, and records would reveal, "between 1883 and 1918 alone the severed body parts of over 80,000 wolves were turned in for bounties."[246] In 1905, a Montana state law was passed requiring veterinarians to infect captured wolves with sarcoptic

---

245   Lopez, 171.
246   Walker, *The Lost Wolves of Japan*, 167–168.

mange and then release the infected wolves in an attempt to spread the disease.[247]

This is western memory. As early as the 1630s, Massachusetts Bay and Virginia instituted wolf bounties, with many US colonies following suit. In 1645, the Massachusetts Bay Colony had formed a committee to "consider of the best ways and means to destroy the wolves which are such ravenous and cruel creatures."[248] Throughout this period, the colonies of Massachusetts Bay, New Plymouth, Virginia, and Rhode Island had all passed legislation rewarding those who killed wolves with payment, in either shillings or live-stock – in other words bounties. Virginia demanded local tribes kill a yearly wolf quota as well,[249] an assertion of dominance over land, wolf, and people who had for many long generations co-existed peaceably, whose land this is, whose land this is still.

And so, the European immigrants recently turned Americans, or Canadians, decimated a continent. The oft-told narrative is of bison disappearing, as if floating off into the ether. By the end of the 1900s, the phenomenal bison herds were nearly extinct. The wolf with them.

That word "disappeared." Its literalness and also opacity.

The Okjökull glacier, the first of Iceland's glaciers to disappear, was given a plaque entitled "A letter to the future":

Ok is the first Icelandic glacier to lose its status as a glacier. In the next 200 years all our glaciers are expected to follow the

247 Flores, *Horizontal Yellow.*
248 Walker, *The Lost Wolves of Japan,* 166.
249 Peterson, *Wolf Nation.*

same path. This monument is to acknowledge that we know what is happening and what needs to be done. Only you know if we did it.[250]

The western population of monarch butterflies is 99 percent gone.[251] Once in a while I see a solitary wanderer, often alone. A core reason: relentless, unmitigated use of pesticides. As with bees. As with myriad ancient insects.

Half of known wildlife extinct within the past 40 years alone! Over a million species now at risk of extinction.

People disappeared, i.e., murdered. Increasingly for standing in the way of land grabs, of open-pit mines, of roads for funneling more timber, more oil, more to market.[252]

Play-ku-tay. Assiniboine word, "the white vandals."[253]

Wasichu. Lakota. "One who takes all the fat."[254]

The controllers will remain the most removed, they will not endure, *until...until...until.*

Bison embody benevolence, strength, and tenacity. The tenacity to survive genocide. Their fate linked to First Peoples, against all odds the bison are returning, alongside the wolves.

250   Emma Taggart, "Scientists Write Eulogy for Iceland's First Glacier Lost to Climate Change," My Modern Met, July 26, 2019, https://mymodernmet.com/lost-iceland-glacier-eulogy/.

251   "Saving the Monarch Butterfly," Center for Biological Diversity, https://www.biologicaldiversity.org/species/invertebrates/monarch_butterfly/.

252   Jonathan Watts, "Murders of Environment and Land Defenders Hit Record High," *The Guardian*, September 13, 2021, https://www.theguardian.com/environment/2021/sep/13/murders-environment-land-defenders-record-high.

253   Savage, *Geography of Blood*, 112.

254   "Wasi'chu," Wikipedia, https://en.wikipedia.org/wiki/Wasi%27chu.

Echo: a battle cry

a five-hundred-year-old curse

a blazing red dawn

ERASED MEMORIES

I grew up in the hills outside the town of Los Osos. Spanish for "The Bears," grizzly bears to be precise. They're long gone now, all but the concrete sculpture of one standing stoic beside the place where Los Osos Creek flows into the Morro Bay estuary. This is the homeland of the yak tityu tityu yak tiłhini Northern Chumash Tribe. This land, and the nearby Pacific Ocean, raised me, formed me, as places do. On Highway 58, back road from Bakersfield through the Carrizo plains to the cowboy town of Santa Margarita, where we used to go as kids for steak at the old saloon, play horse-shoes while the adults drank themselves silly, there is an old aban-doned house still leaning against sun-torched hills. It overlooks oil fields now. Where marshlands used to be. Where grizzly bears used to catch fish. I often imagine what it all used to be. Wolf packs. Massive elk herds. Endless flocks of birds. The Central Valley one great watering hole.

Today, California grasslands in the summer look like sand dunes. Like a beige old mare who loves to kick her hoofs in the water trough, make a noisy splash, and then roll, pleasurably, in the soft dirt. Like the tawny mane of a lion hiding in tall savanna. Like dust. Old California was full of flowers. Wildflowers. In those legendary days, before the Spanish conquistadores came with their horses and cattle, gold lust and gunfire, priests and missions. Wildflowers everywhere, and hill slopes verdant year-round. I've always thought of California as dusty. The California I know.

The Cahuilla word for oak grove, *meki'i'wah*, translates as "the place that waits for me."[255] Many of California's old, gnarled, oak trees stand wide-limbed, hovering over sandy hillsides without a single sapling nearby, no matter how many acorns are dispersed yearly. Barbed wire dissects the land, there are no wolves to keep the herds afoot, and ranchers generally aren't managing for oak regrowth. So, when these old trees eventually crack and fall over, there won't be any mid-sized trees to offer shade for their cows. Oak trees are slow growing. They remind us that there are things we can't just fix without the patience and intelligence of natural time.

One rainy day afternoon, I went to the Oakland Museum of California History. In the science section, there's a stuffed grizzly behind a box of glass, the first thing you see upon entering. Behind the grizzly hangs a California flag, lit up by a bright overhead light. I stood there staring at the two juxtaposed for a long time. The grizzly in the box. The California flag, with its iconic depiction of a grizzly bear, hanging in the background, lamp lit. In Sonoma, at the old mission, most northern of the chain of Spanish missions dotting the California coast, the original flag is on display. Painted in blackberry juice by some timid young soldier tasked to step up as artist, the grizzly looks more like a boar than a bear. It's cute,

---

255   Deborah Small, "What Happens When Native People Lose Their Traditional Foods?" KCET, November 17, 2016, https://www.kcet.org/shows/tending-the-wild/what-happens-when-native-people-lose-their-traditional-foods.

really, taking up a tiny corner section of a huge white cotton sheet. California's first flag.

People think about the fact that grizzly bears are extinct from this state because the bear made it on the flag. There was no mention of wolves in the entire exhibit. I have rarely heard mention of wolves as part of typical California (natural) history. It is an oversight classic to narratives of elimination. Erasure through mute overlook, itself learned and upheld through organizational structures built as deliberately as monuments. Yet you can go to La Brea Tar Pits in Los Angeles and find an exhibit of 400 dire wolf skulls on display, mounted on a tall, yellow-backed wall back lit with warm light. Over 3,600 individual animals have been discovered there, dire wolves the most found mammal in the pits. Because when bison or horses were stuck in the tar asphalt, pursuing wolves would have also become entrapped. This is an example of the land's old memory, revealed to us through bones and fossils, only this was not the end of wolves roaming this land called California, even if to some it may seem so.[256]

In the op-ed, "We Are Still Here. John Muir Is Not," Rebecca Tortes, Jennifer Malone, Leah Mata Fragua, Hillary Renick, A-dae Briones, and Fred Briones propose the following: "Instead of asking how John Muir was racist, perhaps the better question is how the scientific thought that justified those racist behaviors is still actively at the center of the environmental movement?"[257] They describe

256 "Dire Wolves," La Brea Tar Pits & Museum, https://tarpits.org/topics/dire-wolves.
257 Rebecca Tortes, Jennifer Malone, Leah Mata Fragua, Hillary Renick, A-dae Briones, and Fred Briones, "Op-Ed: We Are Still Here. John Muir Is Not," Orion, July 2020, https://orionmagazine.org/2020/08/op-ed-we-are-still-here-john-muir-is-not/.

how the mid-19th-century state university system functioned from a strictly European school of thought. "These standards displaced local knowledge, values, and understandings of the world; it seemed the very nature of being a scientist entailed a disregard and distrust for the generations of knowledge accrued by California's first people." Mentalities rigid with preconceived ideas and hierarchical notions of expertise that continue to this day. "For more context, add the industrial frenzy of the California Gold Rush of 1849, the eugenics movement, the government-sponsored bounty on California Indigenous body parts, and the eighteen secret and unratified treaties."[258]

California. Place of extremes. Pillaged and revered. Logged and dammed and mined and taken. Abundant and exhausted. Edge of the world. End of the line. California, the proverbial whore. California, the life-giving goddess. California, raped. Haunted.

All my life, I've felt the emptiness of   missing.

Today, when California Indigenous People are punished by authorities for gathering roots, basket weaving fibers, preparing foods, and otherwise from their very homelands, "we are being asked to wholly accept an unjust transfer of lands, to forget a history that is ignored by government actors and environmental advocates, and to internalize and bear the burden of a society in which neither we nor our children have rights or access to our own lands."[259] Basket weavers, like wolves, "trespassing" on their own homelands.

The State of California passed a treasury bond law some 30 years prior to Montana's wolf bounty law, only of a different purpose: to pay bounty hunters and state militias to kill Indigenous People. A

258   "We Are Still Here. John Muir Is Not."
259   "We Are Still Here. John Muir Is Not."

- 179 -

law. In the words of Governor Peter H. Burnett, in an address to the state legislature in January 1851: "A war of extermination will continue to be waged between the two races until the Indian race becomes extinct."[260]

Extermination/Extinct.

On the high north archipelago of Svalbard in the Arctic Ocean, midway between continental Norway and the North Pole, bowhead whales still avoid old mating grounds. They live upwards of 200 years and still remember genocide – they do not return to the place where their relatives were slaughtered. And where their blood was spilled, and blubber boiled for lamp oil, lichen the color of rust remains. European whaling companies vied for control of Svalbard's waters during Europe's first "oil rush."[261] This was the beginning of the oil industry.

In the salient words of Joe Rose, Bad River Ojibwe Elder: "We see the wolf as a predictor of our future. What happens to wolf happens to Anishinaabe...whether other people see it or not, the same will happen to them."[262]

260 "Peter Hardeman Burnett," Wikipedia, https://en.wikipedia.org/wiki/Peter_Hardeman_Burnett.
261 Kristin Prestvold, "Svalbard's History," Norwegian Polar Institute, https://cruise-handbook.npolar.no/en/svalbard/history.html.
262 "Ma'iingan (The Wolf) Our Brother."

The autonomy of nonhuman nature seems to me
an indispensable corrective to human arrogance.

—WILLIAM CRONON

WOLVES AND DOGS

"Greenlandic dogs are half-wolf," I was told by Johan, a Greenlander I met at the fishing dock in Nuuk. Different from Canadian huskies and malamutes, he clarified. Johan grew up in Sisimiut, dog sledding. Said he drops his dog pack off on an island in the summer, brings them fish once a week, otherwise they have clean water to drink, and being that it's summer, they don't need much to eat. He said there are 3,000 dogs in Sisimiut alone. There are maybe 50 confirmed wolves in all of Greenland. He acknowledged that his dogs are part wolf.

In Japanese, the words for wolf and mountain dog are blurry, there is not much differentiation between them. The word *oinu*, for instance, "honorable dog," was often used in reference to wolves, when there were wolves.[263] This is in part because of crossbreeding, once popular in Ainu communities in particular because they wanted their dogs to have the hunting skills of wolves. It seems these hybrids were wolves when they were in the mountains but became more dog-like when they were in villages in the company of people.[264]

There now exists a robot dog that can carry 30 pounds and dance; traverse rough terrain in -40–131°F conditions; is equipped

263 Walker, *The Lost Wolves of Japan*, 82.
264 Walker.

with two-way communication but otherwise does not make a sound; and has five depth cameras, in-body force sensors, and various optimization algorithms to move skillfully and track, allowing the human operator 360° vision around the robot in day, or when using night vision.[265] "Spot" is being used by the oil company BP to do inspection work in remote locations, such as oil rigs in the Gulf of Mexico, and to read instrument panels. "Spot" is also called a quad-legged unmanned ground vehicle, or Q-UGV. Manufactured by Ghost Robotics and Immersive Wisdom of Boston Dynamics, who has a long history of making robots for the US Army, they are coined the "installation of the Future."[266] With claims that Q-UGV wolf dogs will never be armed, if someone attempts to steal or otherwise "harm" the robo-wolf, a defense mechanism is triggered. Disclaimers. Unlike actual canines, I don't think they can bite. And yet the Air Force has called them a vital component of the "kill chain."[267] With their long legs, they remind me more of wolves.

When I first learned about the robo-dog, in whom I see a wolf, I saw the whole conundrum embodied in a metal war machine, as well as an oddly twisted hint at that older relationship with wolves. How deeply this is imprinted in our memories, and how fastidiously

265 Oriana Pawlyk, "Robot Security Dogs Have Arrived at Tyndall Air Force Base," Military.com, March 30, 2021, https://www.military.com/daily-news/2021/03/30/robot-security-dogs-have-arrived-tyndall-air-force-base.html.

266 Diana Budds, "The NYPD's New Robot Dog Can't Hurt Us. Yet," New York Magazine, March 4, 2021, https://www.curbed.com/2021/03/nypd-robot-dog-boston-dynamics-spot.html.

267 Brad Lendon, "Robot Dogs Join US Air Force Exercise Giving Glimpse at Potential Battlefield of the Future," CNN, September 9, 2020, https://www.cnn.com/2020/09/09/us/robot-dogs-us-air-force-test-intl-hnk-scli-scn/index.html.

it is misused. Make a robot for war and industry and call it a dog, all the while mimicking a wolf.

Canids have been intimately associated with humans longer than any other animal (excepting primates) on the planet. One of the most telling biological clues to this is shared diseases. Humans share 50 diseases with cattle, for instance, including smallpox, which evolved from cowpox. We share 46 with sheep, 42 with swine, but most of all 65 with canines. Psychologist Caveath Read has argued (echoing Indigenous creation stories) that early people may well have modeled social life after canid packs, that the evolving human mind was "a sort of chimpanzee mind adapted to the wolfish conditions of the hunting pack," and proposes that human's early ancestors should be named *Lycopithecus* – "wolf-ape."[268]

Wolves are not solitary beings. They live in formation, in relation, to this word called "pack," which is another word for family. The lone wolf seeks a partner, a family, a place to call home territory, to know, to return to. *Wolves, it is said, taught people how to live.* Considering the companionship people still have with dogs, the severity of hatred toward wolf is actually rather confounding.

I met a white wolf dog named Ruger in the Black Hills once, while staying in the side cottage of a rental home in Hisega, just outside Rapid City. The owners had adopted the wolf dog because his previous owner, a military man, had up and gone one day due to a change of appointment and left the wolf dog behind. I first saw Ruger upon coming back late one night. Peering up through the corridor between the garage and our cottage, I noticed him standing

268   Flores, *Horizontal Yellow*, 258.

on the deck watching intently through railing slats. A huge, fluffy, long-legged, blizzard-white wolf dog. He didn't make a sound; just cocked his head and met my gaze. His long legs were obviously a wolf's, but he could bark like a dog, even though he was also prone to howl. (Wolves rarely bark, mostly to signal alarm.)

I learned from our host the next day that Ruger was raised by a girl. That the daughter of the guy who'd had Ruger before spent every day with him, roaming around the ponderosa pines, and that once he'd seen the girl asleep atop this wolf dog in the middle of the road, as comfortable as if she were in her own bed.

American writer and historian, and author of *Horizontal Yellow*, Dan Flores, dedicates the last chapter of his book, "Wolf Song Redux," to his experience adopting two wolf hybrids. Flores traveled from West Texas to Alaska for an Arctic tundra wolf and McKenzie River husky cross who had been abandoned in an Anchorage kennel: Wiley. He would later adopt a black wolf he called Ysa, short for *ysambanbi* (Comanche for "handsome wolf). He admits to the impracticality of it, and describes the frequent calls he'd receive from people, like a truck driver in Pampa, Texas, who was looking to get a wolf hybrid to train as a guard-attack animal. When Flores told the guy the simple fact that "animals that were high-percentage wolf were far too shy around people to work as guard dogs," the man hung up on him in disbelief.[269] A kind of disbelief that people hold fast to in order to avoid the effort of having to revise an otherwise particularly simplistic, especially violent, slant of a perspective.

269   Flores, 257.

Ysa and Wiley, while by no means domesticated, were socialized. Meaning they accepted Flores (as alpha) and a small handful of other people (mostly women) but otherwise regarded humans "with abject horror."[270]

For Flores, the decision to take in wolves had more to do with a longing to make real something silenced, to rekindle a worldview suppressed. Had the hills around his West Texas outpost been filled, as they once were, with the nightly echo of howling of wolves, he says he wouldn't have felt so inclined to harbor two wolves in a pen, to relate to them in a context that required a compromised life-style, and compromised the wolves in turn. "The cuddly lamb types (and the ranchers) are right: I suspect that owning wolf hybrids is a symptom of a disturbed personality. What sort of illumination this casts on the wolf in American sense of place could be peripheral, but probably isn't."[271] Flores equates his own yearning to the same summary of loss the wolf symbolizes. "My own experience with wolf hybrids is grounded in a kind of quest for native authenticity in a landscape – the Southern High Plains – that had every last buffalo stripped from it by 1878, every last wolf by 1924, and almost every last blade of grass in my own time." He makes a confession: "I think I have been driven a little crazy by this."[272]

I can relate.

Like the character Chen Zhen from *Wolf Totem*, like Barry Lopez himself, who also adopted wolves and had his own regrets for doing so, it seems people from the dominant cultures seek this forced

270   Flores, 271.
271   Flores, 258.
272   Flores, 258.

pet-owner experience to make up for something lost. Something their ancestors had a hand in destroying.

Wolves are at the core of Flores's questions about identity and the contradictions therein: "The look in those yellow wolf eyes speaks to the heart of the dilemma – of the untamable wildness that frightened Europeans into an orgy of wilderness destruction but also the spirit of a continent that has to be embraced if we are ever going to be Americans."[273]

His words fight against themselves. Untamable wildness/wilderness. Destruction of the spirit of a continent – that was cultivated and cared for, that was *not* wild to the people who lived there. I agree this spirit does need to be embraced, on its own terms. But, again, perhaps part of the problem is the way the word "wild" is used to mean uncontrolled or not obedient. Wolves teach a different kind of relationship.

273   Flores, 256.

^^

Fur 1 black speckled with gold. white blurred by quicksilver. the color of a wet mesa. onyx azure. gray laced with soot, resin, snowflakes. with age more hints of snow. 2 buoyant warmth. tuck nose behind tail, curl up in a tight circle and the ice, the polar wind, are reasonable elements. I am vulnerable in comparison, no thick tail to keep warm by. 3 as hide, used deftly, with regard and care. dishonored in bounty, otherwise sold. that trading post on the way to Thunder Bay, Ontario. one lone stretched out wolf hide hanging by a hook. of the softest fur. I bought a reindeer pelt. rolled it up and crossed back over the border. 4 there is warmth and there is medicine. there is a compass rose called protocol. 5 for years we had a buffalo hide rolled up in a cedar chest, until our son was born and needed cushion, a center place to crawl, sit upright, learn to walk. the first time he stood on two feet, spontaneously and just beside me, I thought he was a bear.

THIS IS THE ESSENCE
OF WOLVES

Farley Mowat, Canadian author of *Never Cry Wolf*, is known for writing things that piss off the establishment. His own experience with wolves started in the Dominion Wildlife Service Finance Department in Ottawa, circa 1950, when from across a dusty desk scattered with yellowing groundhog skulls the chief supervisor states to him: "As you are aware, lieutenant Mowat, the Canis lupus problem has become one of national importance." Wolves were supposedly killing too many deer. When he was hired by the Department of Mines and Resources to "put an end to this intolerable situation,"[274] the wolf was thus assigned Farley Mowat's *problem*. His response to this "problem" made him into a problem. I recognized that word when I read it, reflecting on the times I've had it pinned to my own forehead as well.

As the story goes, that same night Mowat boarded a Canadian Air Force transport plane from Ottawa to Churchill, on the western shore of Hudson Bay. His final destination: somewhere in the subarctic Barren Lands. The equipment he was supplied with included

---

274   Farley Mowat, *Never Cry Wolf* (Toronto: McClelland and Stewart, 1973), 13–14.

things like cookstoves, tents, shotguns, skis, snowshoes, axes, a radio transceiver, and a collapsible canoe, as well as "three great bundles of clanking wolf traps, teargas grenades, smoke generators, and a case of 'wolf getters,' devises which fire potassium cyanide into the mouth of the animal which inspects them."[275]

The orders by which Mowat had been delivered into the bush stated that he conduct a wolf/caribou predator prey survey. He had forgotten about this particular expectation, uncovering a long-neglected Operation Order from under a pile of dirty socks months into his stay in the Barren Lands, and determined rather last minute to do his best to satisfy orders from headquarters. Ootek, a local Inuit man who had become Mowat's friend and guide, and who, Mowat admitted, already knew everything Mowat had come to "study" in Ootek's home terrain, took him upriver by canoe to the tundra plains in the north.

In Mowat's estimation, Ootek spoke wolf language. He understood, for instance, when the wolves got word of the caribou's return. A message that traveled between wolves in neighboring territories. Once Mowat thought Ootek to be humoring him, or crazy, when he took off on a hunting trip so early in the season, until a few days later, when he returned with venison and caribou tongues.[276]

The semi-official estimate of the wolf population of Keewatin, which Mowat had received back in Ontario, based on information from the usual trapper-trader sources, was exaggerated. Mowat is known for exaggerating in his books too, in response to the characteristically detached word of the all-knowing bureaucrat officiating

275 Mowat, 16.
276 Mowat.

from a leather-backed armchair in a musky office, with fastidiously held ideas about places they've never been to. Bureaucrats paid off by the mining companies, the same thing that goes on today. The point of an exaggerated wolf population was to conveniently blame wolves for the decimation of caribou herds, not men with their float planes and rifles. Needless to say, Mowat's wolf/caribou survey flipped headquarters statistics upside down. This didn't matter, of course. Accurate environmental assessments for nation-states won over by big industry rarely do.

The real thing Mowat learned was to know wolves' personhood. So much so that in the final days of his expedition he would face his own inherited assumptions with humble, painful embarrassment.

After months living alongside the pack of wolves Mowat had come to know as individuals and as a family, he realized he still didn't know what the inside of a den looked like. Angeline (his name for the mama wolf of the pack he had lived alongside) and her pups had outgrown the den, so it wasn't currently occupied. So he set off. Within a half-mile of the den, a thunderous roar groaned overhead so jarring that he flung himself onto the mossy ground. It was the pilot returning to Churchill who he'd flagged down earlier to send a message for his retrieval before freeze-up. Startled, he found his way to the den and proceeded to wiggle down the entrance tunnel. With the dim orange glow of a flashlight, he descended at a 45-degree angle for some eight feet, feeling claustrophobic, as the tunnel was just wide enough for him to fit. At the eight-foot mark, the tunnel bent sharply upwards and then swung to the left. He maneuvered, pointing the torch in the new direction and turning the switch back on. Four green lights in the shadows reflected back the dim flash-light beam. Wolves were in the den.

"Despite my close familiarity with the wolf family, this was the kind of situation where irrational but deeply ingrained prejudices completely overmaster reason and experience. To be honest, I was so frightened that paralysis gripped me." The wolves didn't even growl. "Save for the two faintly glowing pairs of eyes, they might not have been there at all." Shoving his flashlight forward he was able to make out Angeline and one of the pups, scrunched against the back wall of the den, frozen still. Shock beginning to wear off, Mowat started to squirm back out of the tunnel, still tense with the fear that the wolves would charge. By the time he emerged, he had not heard or seen the slightest movement from the wolves. Sitting down on a stone and lighting a cigarette, he realized he was no longer frightened but instead overcome with an "irrational rage."[277] He knew that, if he'd had his rifle, he would have undoubtedly reacted in "brute fury and tried to kill both wolves."[278]

Sitting there, with his thoughts and cigarette, he faced his own shame.

I was appalled at the realization of how easily I had forgotten, and how readily I had denied, all that the summer sojourn with the wolves had taught me about them...and about myself. I thought of Angeline and her pup cowering at the bottom of the den where they had taken refuge from the thundering apparition of the aircraft, and I was shamed.

277 Mowat, 174.
278 Mowat, 175.

Somewhere to the eastward a wolf howled; lightly questioning. I knew the voice, for I had heard it many times before. It was George, sounding the wasteland for an echo from the missing members of his family. But for me it was a voice which spoke of the lost world which once was ours before we chose the alien role; a world which I had glimpsed and almost entered...only to be excluded, at the end, by my own self.[279]

Marcus told me about a friend of his who'd gone to work for a summer season in Yellowstone and went for a night hike in the woods once. Alone, with no cell phone, he'd found himself encircled, being watched, by a pack of wolves. This friend said he felt no fear, and that, as ephemerally as the wolves had surrounded him, they disappeared. "That is the essence of wolves," Marcus later reflected, speaking of his own experience at the Cold Meadows guard station on a wildfire assignment and feeling the presence of a wolf pack howling and stalking near to camp, "that of being surrounded, assessed, and then as quickly as they arrive they are gone."[280]

On another fire assignment, he spent a few weeks in the Gila National Forest, New Mexico. One night, he heard wolves howling and felt them circling around their camp. In the morning, he said as much to his crew boss only to be told, "nah, coyotes." Knowing otherwise, he found his way over to the wildlife biologist living nearby in a camper with a very large dog, and sat down a short distance away. She saw him, noticed that he was curious about her dog, and told him, "She's a wolf dog. Don't look at her directly. Look at her out of the

279 Mowat, 174–175.
280 Marcus Lund, personal communication with author, June 2020.

corner of your eyes, and she'll approach you." So he gazed ground-ward, and momentarily the wolf dog was at his side, practically in his lap. While petting her, he mentioned the howling of the previous night. Yes, the biologist had heard it. "They were wolves," she told him plainly, affirmatively. "I know, because if they were coyotes, my dog would have run them off. They were wolves. They were after her. She slept in the camper last night." Wolf dog was torn between being called back, or staying with the woman to whom she felt loyal.

A classmate I attended writing seminars with once shared her story about a furiously starlit night in McCall, Idaho, when she stepped outside the log home her father built on a lot surrounded by pine forests and heard a pack of wolves howling, moving near. Standing outside, beneath the silver light of the moon, Katelyn Newman waited for the wolves to come. Running, the pack split in two around her house and joined back together in the front yard. She watched them pass by her without the slightest glance her way, and spoke of feeling nearly offended at her own insignificance to them.

Mowat writes of a similar realization early on in his stay in the Barren Lands, when he too felt perturbed by wolves' total disregard for his self-assumed obtuse and noteworthy presence. Spooked upon seeing a pair, he'd hidden out near an exposed rock pile while the wolves paid him no attention at all. It was to his disbelief and even, he admits, *incredulous* realization, that they were far more interested in playing tag. When I first read the passage recounting this, it made me laugh out loud.

I once asked Jeannette Armstrong about wolves. She grew up among them in the hills outside the Okanagan Valley in so-called

British Columbia, Canada. She reflected how there are fewer wolves now, like the caribou and the salmon. While Bear, yes, is someone to stay alert toward, as for Wolf: "for us they are like how people tend to view coyotes, just going about their way, nothing to fear."[281]

There was a period of time, when I was perhaps 7 years old, that I reckoned nightly with my fear of death. I'd fall asleep staring out my bedroom window into the obsidian of night punctured by stars, distant and dying, like our Sun. There, alone at the far end of the house, surrounded by miles of oak groves and a steep hill face thick with coyote brush, sometimes interrupted by the hoots of coyotes, I reckoned with death and with infinity. I didn't speak to anyone about this, but night after night I faced off with a great sense of fear, fear of emptiness and the vast unknown. This scared me. It startled me so much that sometimes I'd pull my sheets up over my head, calling on images of happy things: the field of fragrant, multicolored sweet peas planted across from the packing shed, our beloved black ridgeback-Catahoula Dixie, with his stalwart presence and white belly and cuffed paws – anything to conjure away my fear of the unknown.

Fear and how it grips us. How innate, how primal, and also, at times, how fabricated. Mowat at the rock pile. If only we could laugh at ourselves more. And perhaps also face death like Tibetan monks advise us to, as a daily practice, so we might live more fully that day instead. This very reckoning with fear of death is embedded quite deeply in the essence of wolves and in the somewhat inexplicable quality that, while fully capable of killing a human, they very rarely do.

281   Jeannette Armstrong, personal communication with author, September 2019.

He cut down every tree he saw, he shot every animal he saw, he made war on all the people. He made guns to shoot flies with, bullets to shoot fleas with. He was afraid of mountains and made mashers to flatten them, he was afraid of valleys and made fillers to fill them up, he was afraid of grass and burned it and put stones where it was. He was afraid of water, because of the way water is. He tried to use it all up, burying springs, damming rivers, making wells. But if you drink, you piss. Water will come back down. As the desert grows so does the sea. So Little Man poisoned the sea. The fish all died.

(and then)

Coyote came. Where she walked she made the wilderness. She dug canyons, she shat mountains. Under the buzzard's wings forest grew. Where the worm was in the dirt, the spring ran. Things went on, people went on. Only Little Man didn't go on. He was dead. He died of fear.

—URSULA K. LEGUIN, *ALWAYS COMING HOME*

OUTLAW WOLVES

To write about a creature mythic and disappeared is like writing about a shadow, a dream, a fleeting vision of what was, what could yet be.

Robert Shimek writes about Waabishkii-Ma'iingan, Anishinaabe for White Wolf, who appears to assist people in danger. Children escaping from residential school, soldiers in war, a hunter lost in winter.[282] Many of the outlaw wolves, those who evaded trappers' tactics during the days of American conquest, were called spirit wolves by their pursuers. So elusive people took them for spirits. Many were white wolves.

Names of famous rogue wolves, outlaw wolves, spirit wolves, or otherwise, include:

Sycan Wolf of the Sycan Marsh, Oregon
Snowdrift Wolf of Judith Basin
Ghost Wolf of the Little Rockies, Montana
Pine Ridge Wolf and Custer Wolf from South Dakota
Old Whitey of Bear Springs Mesa, Colorado
Three Toes of Harding County, South Dakota

282   Shimek, "The Wolf Is My Brother."

Big Foot, Lane County, Colorado

The Truxton Wolf, Arizona

Lobo, King of Currumpaw, northern New Mexico

Rags the Digger, Cathedral Bluffs, Colorado

The Traveler, west-central Arkansas

Varden Wolf, Virden, Manitoba

Old Lefty, Burns Hole, Colorado

Aquila Wolf, western Arizona

Cody's Captive, Cheyenne, Wyoming

Montana Billy, Medora, North Dakota

Queen Wolf, Unaweep Canyon, Colorado

Black Buffalorunner, Carberry, Manitoba

The Greenhorn Wolf, southern Colorado

Three Toes of the Apishapa, Colorado

Werewolf of Nut Lake, Fort Qu'Appelle, Saskatchewan

Split Rock Wolf, west-central Wyoming

Pryor Creek Wolf, southeastern Montana[283]

These wolves weren't just elusive; they were defiant. They communicated a clear fuck-you to the trappers who sought them. Lobo, the famous Currumpaw wolf, for instance, once gathered up four poisoned baits that had been carefully laid out for him, nudged them into a pile, and defecated on them.[284]

Three Toes, another bandit wolf, a wolf who kept skirting traps and strychnine, bait and bullets, was pursued by over 150 men trying

283   Lopez, *Of Wolves and Men*, 193.
284   Lopez.

to make the kill, all to collect a gold watch offered in reward.[285] I imagine that same gold watch sitting in a pawnshop somewhere now, coated in a film of dust.

There was an old "Wild West" practice that went as follows: lasso a wolf, tie ropes around their neck and paws, then attach the ropes to each respective saddle's pommel so five men on horseback, with conniving grins, can kick their respective horses and ride off in all directions, tearing the wolf apart.

On a Saturday afternoon in Texas, three men rode down a female red wolf and threw a lasso over her neck. When she gripped the rope with her teeth to keep the noose from closing, they dragged her around the prairie until they'd broken all her teeth. Then, while two of them stretched the animal between their horses with ropes, the third man beat her to death with a pair of fence pliers. The wolf was taken around to a few bars in a pickup and finally thrown in a roadside ditch.[286]

People have been murdered like that.

This image: a gang of men with rifles and white, KKK-style masks covering their faces that have draped a dead wolf in an American flag.[287]

To study what people do to wolves is to study what people do to one another.

Wolf killer Ben Corbin is the author of *The Wolf Hunter's Guide: Tells How to Catch 'Em and All About the Science of Wolf Hunting.* Shorthand, it goes by *Corbin's Advice.* Published in 1900, it is a book that premises the wolf war on the grounds of Christianity. For Corbin, guarding

285 Savage, *Wolves.*
286 Lopez, *Of Wolves and Men.*
287 Peterson, *Wolf Nation.*

livestock was part of Divine Providence. "The wolf is the enemy of civilization, and I want to exterminate him."[288]

That word "civilization." The way wolf is an enemy thereof. And yet somehow also oddly revered. Considered a spirit, *spiritual*, by those setting traps, aiming the barrel of their gun to shoot.

In a particularly disturbing account, Corbin writes of having shot a mother wolf while she was fleeing to her den. He then performs a "cesarean operation" to remove her unborn pups from her womb. Claiming to have pulled four "alive and kicking" out from her, he found two more newborn pups in the den. She had been in the process of giving birth when he'd shot her. Then, in a twisted biblical reenactment, he lays all the pups down alongside their dead mother for their "first meals," and according to Scripture, "although you may be dead you yet shall live," he kills them all, hauling their limp bodies away to try and retrieve bounty money.[289] Corbin distinctly, and conveniently, used the flowery language of religion to justify his own violent occupation.

As Barry Lopez has said, "I greatly oversimplify, but there is not much distinction in motive between the Christian missionaries who set fire to England's woods to deprive Druids of a place to worship and the residents of Arkansas who set fire to thousands of acres of the Ouachita National Forest in 1928 to deprive wolves of hiding places."[290]

To study what people do to wolves is to study what people do to one another.

288 Flores, *Horizontal Yellow*, 270.
289 Walker, *The Lost Wolves of Japan*, 137.
290 Lopez, *Of Wolves and Men*, 141–142.

I sat in the Williston Walmart parking lot one cold North Dakota night in the midst of the recent oil boom. Windows slowly fogged up by the breath of conversation, my view of shadowed men and big trucks, an *entire* parking lot full of wayward oilmen and their vehicles, slowly fogged from view. I wouldn't have even considered opening the car door and walking into the store alone. Stories at the time were of men hiding out behind oversized trucks with a knife in hand to slit the Achilles heel on a woman in passing and rape her. Women disappearing, especially Indigenous women. Violence against woman trails extractive industries, as radioactive socks are tossed into ditches and unlisted frack chemicals are pumped into the underground, women are abused, trafficked, killed. MMIW: missing and murdered Indigenous women. Their names cover 90 pages.[291]

To study what people do to wolves is to study what people do to one another, and to the land.

Frack fields *devastate*: A verb that harkens back to the 1630s, for "lay waste, ravage, make desolate." Although, apparently not common until the 19th century.[292] When I looked the word up, I noticed how it was not much used until the industrial boom era.

Dick Cheney made fracking fluid exempt from the Clean Water Act.[293] Alongside serving as secretary of defense, and then vice president of the United States, Cheney was also CEO of the

291 Tony Rehagen, "Their Names Cover 90 Pages," Poetry Foundation, October 8, 2018, https://www.poetryfoundation.org/articles/148001/their-names-cover-90-pages.

292 "Devastate (v.)," Online Etymology Dictionary, https://www.etymonline.com/word/devastate.

293 "The Halliburton Loophole," Earthworks, https://earthworks.org/issues/inadequate_regulation_of_hydraulic_fracturing/.

multinational Halliburton, a company responsible for most of the world's fracking operations. Jack Dalrymple, North Dakota's governor at the time, shepherded in the oil boom. In other words, organized crime. Men with license plates from every state in the nation, including Alaska, arriving on two-lane highways that used to see maybe one car per hour. Deer, elk, moose, and migrating birds killed ceaselessly by revving truckers. Gas flares the size of six-story buildings blazing all day, all night, for over a decade now. Ongoing. The flaring hasn't stopped. Groundwater recklessly polluted. For how many generations? And, in the end, when all the pumps were set in place, the boom became a bust. Oil money typically extracted, no funds left to clean up the mess, locals left to live with it.

To study wolves is to consider that the metaphor of Wolf has far more to do with people than wolves, and humanity's propensity toward control, destruction, violence, and greed. Wolves live on. Even when they die, they show us ourselves.

Ernest Thompson Seton's 1898 book *Wild Animals I Have Known* opens with the story about Lobo and Blanca of the Currumpaw pack. Seton, like Leopold, started out as a wolfer. Of English and Scottish immigrant parents, he grew up in Toronto, Ontario. Tempted by the $1,000 bounty on Lobo's head, posted by ranchers of the Cross L Ranch in the Currumpaw Valley of New Mexico, Seton tried his hand. Lobo was smart to the poison bait and traps, so Seton got smart to Lobo and who Lobo cared for, which was Blanca. Seton focused on baiting Blanca instead. He trapped and killed her. With his mate gone, Lobo howled for days. In mourning, he let himself be trapped also. Seton tied Lobo up beside his cabin, unable to shoot him, but Lobo refused the water Seton left for him. Seton trapped Lobo through heartbreak. Lobo chose to die.[294]

After watching Lobo die, something broke for Seton, like Leopold. For the rest of his life, he too went from trapper to wolf and wilderness advocate.

The question I find myself sitting with is this: What gets lost when such lessons have to come so hard? When wolves are made into spirits, sought, and then revered in their absence.

294 Ernest Thompson Seton, *Wild Animals I Have Known* (New York: Charles Scribner's Sons, 1898).

In the end, the essence of the meaning of the word "wild" is an unknowable, at least partly because the moment it is known, it is no longer wild...We must therefore, when we describe a place or an animal as wild, mean something more than merely undomesticated, or uninhabited by humans, but having also some undescribed, possibly indescribable, essence that is present, of another dimension perhaps, something that cannot be known without destroying it, or that cannot be known at all.

—SHARON BUTALA, *WILD STONE HEART*

RETURN

The first wolf to return to California crossed the state line in the fall of 2011. He was a gray wolf from northeastern Oregon who had set off southbound. Over the course of the coming months, he would travel over 2,000 miles searching for a mate. His name: OR-7. Lucky number seven. *OR* signifying his state of origin, 7 marking him as the seventh wolf to be radio-collared so he could be monitored by satellite and a computer link as part of the Imnaha pack, from which he came. One of the first wolf packs to establish themselves in Oregon's recent history, after the last known wolf killed for bounty, in 1946.[295]

The first wolf to return to Oregon arrived in 1999. She traveled to the Blue Mountains in the northeast, crossing over from Idaho, but was promptly captured and returned. Between 2000 and 2007, three more wolves were found in northeastern Oregon, two of them shot, all dispersing from Idaho.[296]

In the town of Joseph, in Wallowa County, Oregon, the local sporting goods shop displays posters that read, "Zero Tolerance for Canadian Wolves," followed by claims that wolves are an invasive

295 "Wolves on the West Coast," Center for Biological Diversity, http://www.biologicaldiversity.org/campaigns/wolves_on_the_west_coast/.
296 Moskowitz, *Wolves in the Land of Salmon.*

species that have decimated elk populations in Idaho and would damn sure do the same in Oregon. A "Wallowa County Wolf Defense Fund" has been set up to provide legal fees for people who "shoot wolves in personal defense," or otherwise "in defense of personal property."[297]

For OR-7, wearing the radio collar meant people could track him. Scientists, school children, and poachers alike. Some wolves will physically reject collars; chew them off of one another. In this case, the attention OR-7 got as a lone wanderer tracking south, surviving a long journey past plenty of people who would have liked to kill him, made him into a kind of mythic journeyman who wasn't mythic any longer but home.

The saga started in September 2011 when, at 2 years old, OR-7 left, traveling along the Wallowa Mountains, down through eastern Oregon, circling the lapis lazuli blue of Crater Lake, and then turning west into the Cascade Mountains. Three months later, he crossed the state line into California in late December of that same year, the first wolf to return to California since 1924, being the year the last documented California wolf was shot in Lassen County.[298] Of all places, he spent that summer of 2012 amid Lassen Volcanic National Park and in the Plumas National Forest.

Into the spring of 2013, his radio collar started dying out, and for his own protection the biologists decided to refrain from attempting to recollar him. Blackout. People didn't know where he was any longer. Then, in May 2014, he was seen on camera with an

---

297   Moskowitz, 202–203.
298   "Wolves on the West Coast."

ebony mate. They would return to Oregon to have their pups in the Oregon Cascades.[299]

It was on a lonesome stretch of road in the Alberta high plains on the way to Head-Smashed-In Buffalo Jump when I learned about the first wolf pack to return to Northern California. What would become known as the Shasta pack. Following OR-7's lead, this was the first wolf pack to cross the border into California hinterlands after nearly a century. Being in the Great Plains when I read this news felt appropriate. The land we were crossing over was once a dense tapestry of prairie, with thundering bison herds, grizzly bears, vast bird migrations, myriad calico insects, and wolves. A pack of black wolves had just returned home, slipping across the Oregon border into Modoc County. I beamed.

As of 2020, there were over a dozen wolves living in California. Wolves are returning to European countries, where they've been gone going on 200 years. From Poland into eastern Germany. Crossing the Alps from Italy into southern France. Photographed trotting across a road in the Netherlands. The first litter of pups filmed on the Danish mainland. Trespassing the mountains between Norway and Sweden.[300]

What does *return* mean amid the sixth mass extinction?

What *if* the word "wild" meant *home*?

299 Peterson, *Wolf Nation*.
300 Michelle Nijhuis, "The Most Political Animal," *The Atlantic*, April 17, 2019, https://www.theatlantic.com/science/archive/2019/04/norway-divided-over-countrys-wolves/587302/.

I know perfectly well that we may all die, and relatively soon, in a global holocaust, which was first imprinted, probably against their wishes, on the hearts of the scientist fathers of the atomic bomb, no doubt deeply wounded and frightened human beings; but I also know we have the power, as all the Earth's people do, to conjure up the healing rain imprinted on Black Elk's heart. Our death is in our hands.

But what I'm sharing with you is this thought: The Universe responds. What you ask of it, it gives. The military-industrial complex and its leaders and scientists have shown more faith in this reality than have those of us who do not believe in war and who want peace. They have asked the Earth for all its deadlier substances. They have been confident in their faith in hatred and war. The Universe ever responsive, the Earth ever giving, has opened itself fully to their desires.

—ALICE WALKER

THE RED FOREST
IS GREEN AGAIN

Chernobyl: the world's largest nuclear meltdown. Over 50,000 people evacuated because of an invisible substance that would have killed them slowly and violently if they'd stayed. Wind currents carry radioactive fallout across Europe, it settles into fields, lichen, rivers, oceans, and seas. The center area, where the plumes were thickest and settled most heavily into the ground, is a place referred to as "The Zone."

This is the same place that was once called the Red Forest, for the way the trees all turned a rust red color after the meltdown. Today, the trees are verdant again. The color of jade. Their bark highly contaminated, of course, as is the soil underfoot. The highest risk of radiation is in the dust.

Researchers and rangers who patrol the area to keep an eye out for poachers who go after the wild horses and to track wolves to count their growing number are given limited periods of time to enter the center of the Zone. The entirety is an area of nearly 1,000 square miles. One must be especially careful on a windy day, or if digging in the soil.

Chernobyl today is a place with no human residents (aside from a motley assortment of undaunted trespassers, also known as "stalkers").[301] Instead, it has become a refuge for animals: bison, deer, moose, beaver, fox, raven, wild horse, and wolf.

The bison were reintroduced from Belarus when people began to see this place as a kind of post-apocalyptic national park. The wolves came on their own. They've taken over abandoned villages, climbing atop snow-crusted rooftops in mid-winter to get a good view. Making a wolf pup crib in an old potato cellar.

They are not alone in doing so. Eagles nest in the fire towers in winter, and storks have made nests in deserted cemeteries where bright pink and orange plastic flowers hang. (People are allowed a visit to their dead relatives once a year.) An abandoned factory also offers convenient shelter for wolves in the deep winters. And the ghost city of Prypyat has raptors nesting in apartment buildings. A researcher will climb the paint-chipped hallway stairs to a vacant balcony on the eighth or fifteenth floor, where a tidy twig nest sits in the corner full of fluffy, squeaking, baby hawks.

These tower blocks give a view of the reactor. They were once home to the scientists and engineers who worked at the nuclear facility. The city is overgrown now, green devouring cement gray. In the waters beneath the reactor itself, eight-feet-long giant catfish swim leisurely. They are huge because they are old, not obviously deformed.

The return of wolves as top predators signals that if they can survive, other animals can also. The work of investigating wolves in this off-limits place involves caution; danger lies in the chance of

301   Markiyan Kamysh, *Stalking the Atomic City: Life among the Decadent and the Depraved of Chornobyl* (New York: Astra Publishing House, 2022).

swallowing even a single wolf hair. That much would poison a person. Otherwise, carrying a drowsy wolf to an open clearing to collar requires a little extra protection, gloves for good measure.

Still, researchers carry a bright-yellow, hand-held box to detect radiation. It goes off with a loud and persistent beep when run against the fur of a wolf. Their bones, like the tree bark, are full of radiation. Nevertheless, they have found that wolves are now being born even in the center of the Zone. Dormice are also reproducing here, with some defects, but overall their populations are strong and growing.

This is the inexplicable piece of the story: animals are thriving.

When I was 19, I worked at the Opearen pub in Christiania, a renegades' community smack in the center of Copenhagen that used to flaunt an open market with vendors selling spliffs and bars of hash that looked like chocolate. Pushers and locals, sometimes tourists, would gather around barrel fires in the dirt streets on cold nights. A duvet of clouds hid even the moon, as well as the sun, for weeks on end. Boris worked as the sound guy. He had a stoic presence and a perpetual cigarette that coiled smoke while he managed the switch dial; he was as steady as the unwavering overcast sky. I got to know him, and his rowdy Russian comrades, heard his stories of Mother Russia. I argued with him about Chernobyl once, stunned when he'd told me there is no issue there: it's not like they say, people are fine and basically the whole nuke accident was a propaganda scam. I would later learn he had a point, but only if speaking of catfish and wolves.

At the heart of the Zone, the Pripyat River is ten miles wide. It now floods abandoned villages and fields because the dikes are no longer in use. The waterway is free to move with naturally unpredictable contours. Beavers have also returned in greater numbers and are transforming the channelized canals into marshes. Orchards still blossom and fruit, food for wild boar, deer, and birds. The story here before the meltdown was of classic agrarian-industrial progress. Cut down the forests, plow the fields, and kill off the free-roaming animals.

There is no explanation as to how the health and revival of herds and packs in a terrain drenched in radioactive fallout is possible, but apparently it is. And it is a rather beautiful irony; an example of what is possible, even in the seemingly worst-case scenario, when people stop. At least when people stop taking the land for all it's worth. Because people are not gone, even from the heart of the Zone, and that is important to remember.

It is people who returned bison back to the Great Plains when they saw the possibility of renewal born out of devastation. It is people – adept researchers who have learned to howl like a wolf, keep an eye on packs and count litters of pups, and collect stray hairs to study – who try and conceive of how renewal is possible in circumstances that have otherwise made it impossible for people to live there.[302] It is too simple to say people are the problem. But the metaphors people live by matter and determine how one chooses to live.

If anything, this post-Chernobyl meltdown saga stares in the face of human arrogance, which says, "We are killing the planet," when we are not capable of that. Nor are we positioned to "save the planet" either. People are, of course, capable of creating the conditions for extinction and compromising all for future generations. People are also perfectly capable of shutting up, sitting down on the solid earth, and

---

302   "Radioactive Wolves," *Nature*, season 30, episode 1, October 18, 2011, http://www.pbs.org/wnet/nature/radioactive-wolves-full-episode/7190/.

listening to those who know how to nurture renewal, which inevitably means living by different guiding metaphors, different stories.

Combined, the world's so-called nuclear powers (i.e., nation-state governments) with this strange technology in the form of bombs have detonated more than 500 nukes into the atmosphere. Done as tests to demonstrate mastery and puff up like roosters against rival nations. Recent research shows that honey across the United States contains the fallout of these adolescent demonstrations. Previous research after the Chernobyl disaster showed elevated levels of cesium in European honey and pollen as well. Whether or not research proved or proves this in one defined country or another, the reality is global. Thanks to westerlies and rain, bombs detonated in the Marshall Islands and the US southwest spread across the entire planet. Chernobyl fallout has contaminated the lichen reindeer eat across the Arctic and beyond.

Cesium, similar in structure to potassium, makes it familiar to plants. Plants thus absorb cesium, and bees – who we profoundly depend upon – collect pollen from flowering plants. In other words, they pollinate the manifold food crops we depend on. If the honey is "considered safe for human consumption," this means the bees are suffering. Add in the relentless chemical rain of pesticides and seeming unending loss of habitat, but also the ripple effects of nuclear radiative fallout. [303]

303   Matthew Gault, "American Honey Is Radioactive from Decades of Nuclear Bomb Testing," Motherboard, April 22, 2021, https://www.vice.com/en/article/5dbzan/american-honey-is-radioactive-from-decades-of-nuclear-bomb-testing.

Most nuclear bomb detonations ceased in 1963 with the Limited Nuclear Test Ban Treaty.[304] However, this is akin to the saga of plastic breaking down in the oceans, lakes, rivers, and now showing up in the rain. Or, otherwise, carbon dioxide, methane, and pollution building up in the atmosphere. Or the veritable ring of space junk orbiting our planet, no telling how it is affecting the equator. The real fallout happens generations after life-defying decisions take place.

In *A Chorus of Stones: The Private Life of War*, American author Susan Griffin describes how a chain reaction – the chemistry by which the atom bomb was made – destroys the interconnectedness of the matrix. Neutrons bombard atoms, atoms in turn release other neutrons that bombard other atoms, and so dismantle the entire system of relation. In other words: explosion. "By the same discovery through which science has finally learned that the enspiriting force and matter are one, science has also discovered a way to separate energy from matter, rending apart thus the fabric that we now know holds existence together."[305]

Some ten miles as the crow flies from land I call home, there is a nuclear power plant appropriately named El Diablo. California is known for earthquakes, and seismologists have located several fault lines a few miles off the coast from where radioactive waste is stored underground. On the power lines that traverse the valley between our old dirt road and Los Osos Creek, PG&E has tacked up sirens. They hang there, white as a toilet bowl, a reminder. Should those sirens ever start blaring, it means one thing: run and never come back.

---

304 Gault.
305 Susan Griffin, *A Chorus of Stones: The Private Life of War* (New York: Doubleday, 1992), 80.

It is unknown what it means if wolves travel past the boundaries of the Zone and breed with wolves whose fur is not radioactive. It is unknown what the buildup of radioactivity in honey, pesticides in water, and decayed plastics in soil will do to our children's children. To their capacity to bear children. It is unknown what the fission reactions starting to act up again will mean at Chernobyl, or our many other deteriorating nuclear power plants. Not to mention war.

We endure. And the center of planet Earth, a molten core Hawai'ians know as Goddess Pele, still rises on occasion to remind us of forces greater than ourselves.

Center Point

<><.><>

On this day
in the center
of this universe
walk across
sagebrush flats
into arroyo
past the open
pit coal mine
and truck stop
with that lightning
cracked cottonwood
follow the sound
of howl toward
calving grounds
the air salted
clouds braid
and unbraid
carve rivers
into canyons
explode

<><.><>

THE METAPHOR OF WOLF

Sköll ("one who mocks") and Hati ("one who hates")[306] in the old Norse tongue are the names of two wolves mentioned in passing in *The Prose Edda* by Icelandic poet and historian Snorri Sturluson.[307] One of the wolves chases the moon, the other the sun. Chariot drivers pulled by four horses motion Sun and Moon in transit across the sky, and it is the pursuing wolves who keep them moving, who ensure the consistent and seemingly never-ending rhythm of day to night. Until the wolves devour the chariot drivers and their glowing orbs, foretold as Ragnarök, when the world ends. In the words of English author A.S. Byatt, in her own telling of this saga: "Wind Time, Wolf Time, before the World breaks up."[308]

People interpreting this ancient Eddic poem assume Fenrir is the father, trickster god Loki's wolf-son, but the word in reference, Hróðrsvitnir, means "famous wolf," so it is not unequivocally him. People also infer these wolves are siblings, a brother and sister, and although some are sure Sköll chases the moon and Hati the sun,

306 Daniel McCoy, "Skoll and Hati," Norse Mythology for Smart People, https://norse-mythology.org/skoll-hati/.

307 Snorri Sturluson, *The Prose Edda: Norse Mythology*, trans. Jesse L. Byock (London: Penguin Books, 2005).

308 A.S. Byatt, *Ragnarok* (Edinburgh, UK: Canongate Books, 2019), 135.

poetry has a way of leaving things uncertain, mysterious. It would be easy to portray these wolves as ravenous, murderous, the ones to blame should the world end.[309] Yet is it really that simple? I see the wolves and chariot drivers, the people, as integrally related, together keeping sync. Sunrise to moonrise. And I wonder if perhaps that is what we must remember should we want to stave off the world's end.

Facts about the world as we know it ending don't often win out. People are drowning in facts, have become numb toward them. Facts about ecological collapse, toxic air pollution, political corruption, melting glaciers, war crimes, relentless corporate immunities, unprecedented economic injustice, microplastics in our drinking water, microplastics in, well, everything. Ever more downtrodden facts are also annoying when the structural conditions remain, when the key decision makers still look the same, when they say one thing and do another. So when people rise to confront the forces perpetuating demise, it is because of something deeper than the fact that one needs water to survive. It is the reckoning that water *is* alive, that water is life. A poetic reckoning that is metaphorical, abundant with meaning.

A-dae Romero Briones shared a word from her mother tongue, Keres, with me one day. A word I found could only be written down in translation multidirectionally, like a compass rose:

309   McCoy, "Skoll and Hati."

Ya

Center of being   .   Point of Creation

a word that means all at once:

Mother

Land

How we relate as people[310]

The understanding of Wolf as guide took on new meaning for me as a mother. To become another's guide and protector for a crucial period of time. To be living in a world so bereft of guidance and common sense protection of life. In a time of war against life itself, a brutal inheritance. As is embedded in the meaning of Ya, to care for another – whether one's child or the land one lives upon – is made strong in how we relate, in reciprocal relationship. We are guided and protected by our children in return. We are cared for by the land and all that this word encompasses – the threadwork of life.

My son's generation is growing up in an era when people from his grandparents' generation have told me, more times than I'd like to count, "I'm glad I'll be gone." These same people have otherwise pitied my own generation, declaring that it's up to us to make things right. As for our children, the pity has grown wide-eyed, with an edge of terror glossed over by denial. I have wanted to say in response, each time and over again, "Well, why do you insist on taking

310   A-dae Romero Briones, personal communication with author, May 2021.

the world with you when you go?" These are the words and actions of people perhaps less from a singular generation than more from a particular class, being comfortably removed from all that has been wrong for a very long time.

Amid forces willingly ransacking life to no end, the sixth mass extinction well underway, economic forces that function like a war machine, and amid the realness of blatant war, daring to trust that life will prevail is perhaps in itself a form of rebellion. Because to trust this is to act accordingly – to walk another path.

The ongoing fight of Earth ethos versus evangelical industrialization is a fight over worldview. Yet the choice is not an easy duality, not simply between the notion of Wolf as heroine or Wolf as devil. It is rather to reckon that Wolf exists intelligently, and we exist also, and moreover that our capacity for wisdom and well-being is intertwined. Wolf herself, and also Wolf as metaphor.

Grandmother Wolf kicks her head back and howls. Others join in from across the valley. One by one, they accompany her. Sounds vary. Octaves differ. Each voice distinct. The howling echoes, resonating. Pups join in mimicking; they are training. "What does it mean?" people wonder. "What are they saying?" people ask. Grandmother Wolf just wants to sing.

echo

echo

echo

echo

Selected Sources

Al-Mohaimeed, Yousef. *Wolves of the Crescent Moon*. New York: Penguin Books, 2003.

Antonelli, Lenny. "Lay of the Land: In the Ghost Wood." *Orion*, Spring 2021.

Arke, Pia. *Ethno-Aesthetics/Etnoæstetik*. Copenhagen, Denmark: ARK, 1995.

Askins, Renee. *Shadow Mountain*. New York: Anchor Books, 2013.

Bird Rose, Deborah. *Dingo Makes Us Human: Life and Land in an Aboriginal Australian Culture*. Cambridge, UK: Cambridge University Press, 1992.

Brody, Hugh. *The Other Side of Eden: Hunters, Farmers, and the Shaping of the World*. New York: North Point Press, 2001.

Byatt, A.S. *Ragnarok*. Edinburgh, UK: Canongate Books, 2019.

Calvez, Leigh. *The Breath of a Whale*. Seattle: Sasquatch Books, 2019.

Craighead George, Jean. *Julie of the Wolves*. New York: HarperCollins Publishers, 1972.

—. *Julie's Wolf Pack*. New York: HarperCollins Publishers, 1997.

Davis, Elizabeth. *Heart & Hands: A Midwife's Guide to Pregnancy & Birth*. 4th Edition. Berkeley, CA: Celestial Arts, 2004.

Davis, Elizabeth, and Debra Pascali-Bonaro. *Orgasmic Birth: Your Guide to a Safe, Satisfying and Pleasurable Birth Experience*. Emmaus, PA: Rodale Books, 2010.

Dutcher, Jim, and Jamie Dutcher. *The Hidden Life of Wolves*. Washington, DC: National Geographic Society, 2013.

Eisenberg, Cristina. *The Wolf's Tooth: Keystone Predators, Trophic Cascades, and Biodiversity*. Washington, DC: Island Press, 2013.

Flores, Dan. *Horizontal Yellow: Nature and History in the Near Southwest*. Albuquerque: University of New Mexico Press, 1999.

Frazer, Sir James George. *The Golden Bough*. New York: Macmillan Publishing, 1922.

Gammage, Bill. *The Biggest Estate on Earth: How Aboriginees Made Australia*. Sydney, Australia: Allen & Unwin, 2014.

Gonzales, Patrisia. *Red Medicine: Traditional Indigenous Rites of Birthing and Healing*. Tucson: The University of Arizona Press, 2012.

Greve, Anniken. *Sámi Stories: Art and Identity of an Arctic People*. Tromsø, Norway: Orkana akademisk, 2014.

Griffin, Susan. *A Chorus of Stones: The Private Life of War* (New York: Doubleday, 1992).

Hausman, Gerald. *Turtle Island Alphabet: A Lexicon of Native American Symbols and Culture*. New York: St. Martin's Press, 1993.

Huffman, Julia. *Medicine of the Wolf*. Cleveland, OH: Gravitas Ventures, 2015. eVideo.

Kamysh, Markiyan. *Stalking the Atomic City: Life among the Decadent and the Depraved of Chornobyl*. New York: Astra Publishing House, 2022.

Kapil, Bhanu. *Humanimal: A Project for Future Children*. Berkeley, CA: Kelsey Street Press, 2009.

Kimmerer, Robin. "Speaking of Nature." *Orion*, March/April 2017. https://orionmagazine.org/article/speaking-of-nature/.

LaDuke, Winona. *How to Be a Water Protector*. Halifax, NS: Fernwood Press, 2000.

Lakoff, George, and Mark Johnson. *Metaphors We Live By*. Chicago: The University of Chicago Press, 1980.

Leopold, Aldo. *A Sand County Almanac*. London: Oxford University Press, 1949.

Lopez, Barry. Foreword to *Earthly Love: Stories of Intimacy and Devotion from Orion*. By Alex Carr Johnson, Kathleen Dean Moore, and Teddy Macker. Great Barrington, MA: Orion Society, 2020.

—. *Of Wolves and Men*. New York: Scribner, 1978.

Louv, Richard. *Last Child in the Woods: Saving Our Children from Nature-Deficit Disorder*. Chapel Hill, NC: Algonquin Books of Chapel Hill, 2005.

Marmon Silko, Leslie. *The Turquoise Ledge: A Memoir*. New York: Penguin, 2011.

—. *Yellow Woman and a Beauty of the Spirit*. New York: Simon & Schuster, 2014.

Moskowitz, David. *Wolves in the Land of Salmon*. Portland, OR: Timber Press, 2013.

Mowat, Farley. *Never Cry Wolf*. Toronto: McClelland and Stewart, 1973.

Mt. Pleasant, Jane. "The Paradox of Plows and Productivity: An Agronomic
     Comparison of Cereal Grain Production under Iroquois Hoe Culture and
     European Plow Culture in the Seventeenth and Eighteenth Centuries."
     Agricultural History 85, no. 4 (Fall 2011): 460–492.
Niemeyer, Carter. *Wolf Land*. Boise, ID: BottleFly Press, 2016.
Norwegian Institute for Nature Research (NINA). *The Fear of Wolves: A Review
     of Wolfs Attacks on Humans*. A Large Carnivore Initiative for Europe.
     Trondheim, Norway: NINA, January 2002. http://www.nina.no/archive/
     nina/PppBasePdf/oppdragsmelding/731.pdf.
Ohiyesa. "First Impressions of Civilization." *Harper's Monthly Magazine*,
     March 1904.
okpik, dg nanouk. *Corpse Whale*. Tucson: The University of Arizona Press, 2012.
Peterson, Brenda. *Wolf Nation: The Life, Death and Return of Wild American
     Wolves*. Philadelphia, PA: Da Capo Press, 2017.
Pinkola Estés, Clarissa. *Women Who Run with the Wolves*. New York: Ballantine
     Books, 1992.
Rong, Jiang. *Wolf Totem*. New York: Penguin Books, 2008.
Rudner, Ruth. *A Chorus of Buffalo*. Short Hills, NJ: Burford Books, 2000.
Savage, Candace. *Geography of Blood*. Vancouver, BC: Greystone Books, 2012.
—. *Wolves*. Vancouver, BC: Douglas & McIntyre, 1995.
Seton, Ernest Thompson. *Wild Animals I Have Known*. New York: Charles
     Scribner's Sons, 1898.
Shepard, Paul. *Nature and Madness*. Athens: University of Georgia Press, 1998.
Sturluson, Snorri. *The Prose Edda: Norse Mythology*. Translated by Jesse L.
     Byock. London: Penguin Books, 2005.
Teara: The Encyclopedia of New Zealand. *Story: Papatūānuku – the land*.
     https://teara.govt.nz/en/papatuanuku-the-land/page-4.
Van Tighem, Kevin. *The Homeward Wolf*. Victoria, BC: Rocky Mountain
     Books, 2013.
Walker, Brett. *The Lost Wolves of Japan*. Seattle: University of Washington
     Press, 2009.

Index

Flores, Dan, 185–86, 187
Forest Spirit, 156
Foster, Tonya, 151
fracking, 201–2
Fragua, Leah Mata, 178–79
freedom, 99
fur, 84, 188

G
Germany, 24
ghada, 52
Gianforte, Greg, 23–24
Goddess Pele, 215
Gonzales, Patrisia, 57–58
Gourd Dance, 49–50
Great Plains, 136, 170
Great Seal of the Pawnee Nation, 15
Greek mythology, 48
Greenland, 77–78, 100, 118, 121
 dogs, 182
 Kalaallisut, 77
 wolves, 21
grizzly bears, 176–77
Guardian, 87
guerilla warfare, 136

H
Haber, Gordon, 65–67, 124–25
Halberstam, Jack, 101
Halliburton, 201
The Hammer of Witches, 55
hand signs, 15
Harper's Monthly, 132
Havasupi, 144
Hayao Miyazaki, 156
Hegelund, Liisi Egede, 77, 78
Hegewa, Bert, 47
hide hunters, 172
Hill, Lilian, 70
Himalayan wolf, 138
Hirpini People of Italy, 48

Hitler, 140. *See also* Wolf's Lair
Holy Eagle, Sonja, 130
Holy Inquisition, 56
Horizontal Yellow (Flores), 185–86
Hornaday, William T., 153
hound dogs, 148–49
Humanimal (Kapil), 50–51
hunting, 19–20

I
Indigenous People, 94, 133
 bison and, 171
 California, 179–80
 colonialism and, 57–58, 86–87
 exile, 171
 languages and lexicon, 68, 73–75
 women, 201
 See also specific tribe
International Monetary Fund, 88, 89
International Wolf Center, 21
In the Blank Page I See a Snowdrift,
 164–67
intuition, 78
Inuit People, 131–32
Inupiat, 27
Iowa, 172
Irish Folklore Trilogy (Moore), 155
Iroquois agriculture, 97
 Euro-American farmers, 97
 maize, 97

J
Japan, 22–23, 40–44
 industrial recovery, 44
 Meiji government, 42–44
 Meiji Restoration of 1868, 41, 42
 pollution disaster, 44
 Satchō alliance, 42
 words for wolf and mountain dog, 182
 See also Ainu
Jiang Rong. *See* Lu Jiamin

ABOUT THE AUTHOR

Sonja Swift is a writer and poet of hybrid forms.
She has published a range of poems, as well as various articles
and photo essays. Alumna of California College of the Arts,
she is the author of *Alphabet Atlas*, a chapbook of prose poems
published by Deconstructed Artichoke Press, and *Tarot of
Transformation*, a series of vignettes published by True Story.
Sonja is Danish American and comes from dusty, sometimes
emerald, coastal hills amid a chain of old volcanic peaks that
stretch into the Pacific Ocean. *Echo Loba, Loba Echo:
Of Wisdom, Wolves, and Women* is her first book.